AVOIDING
LEGAL
HASSLES

SUCCESSFUL SCHOOLS
Guidebooks to Effective
Educational Leadership
Fenwick W. English, Series Editor

AVOIDING LEGAL HASSLES

What School

Administrators

Really *Need*

to Know

William A. Streshly
Larry E. Frase

CORWIN PRESS, INC.
A Sage Publications Company
Newbury Park, California

For information address:

Corwin Press, Inc.
A Sage Publications Company
2455 Teller Road
Newbury Park, California 91320

SAGE Publications Ltd.
6 Bonhill Street
London EC2A 4PU
United Kingdom

SAGE Publications India Pvt. Ltd.
M-32 Market
Greater Kailash I
New Delhi 110 048 India

LB2805
. S8x
Vol.3
Cop.2

Printed in the United States of America

Library of Congress Cataloging-in-Publication Data

Streshly, William A.
 Avoiding legal hassles: what school administrators really need to know / William A. Streshly, Larry E. Frase.
     p.   cm.—(Successful schools; v. 3)
 Includes bibliographical references (p.).
 ISBN 0-8039-6018-2 (pb)
     1. School management and organization—United States.
 2. Educational law and legislation—United States. I. Frase, Larry
 E. II. Title. III. Series.
 LB2801.A2S77 1992   92-5995
 371.2′00973—dc20   CIP

92 93 94 95 10 9 8 7 6 5 4 3 2 1

Corwin Press Production Editor: Tara S. Mead

Contents

Foreword

The first time a parent threatened to sue me when I was a school superintendent, I shuddered. I didn't know if that threat could be made real and I would be humiliated in some courtroom under cross-examination by Perry Mason before a bemused jury.

Lawsuits are a fact of life for school administrators. Schools are contested places for some of the most important guarantees in American life. That's why so many lawsuits revolve around the Bill of Rights. Lawyers who specialize in constitutional law covet an opportunity to represent school students and their parents in the inevitable courtroom brouhahas that often result in titanic battles that define our basic freedoms. One thinks immediately of the cases involving Bible reading, free speech, and dissent from sanctioned political practices (as when some groups were protected from compulsory schooling in the case of the Amish or saluting the flag in the case of Jehovah's Witnesses).

An understanding of school law continues to be of critical importance if one is to remain successful as a school administrator in America. I am reminded of that each time I advise foreign students in setting up their programs in educational administration.

No one can appreciate American public education without an adequate grounding in our legal system and, in turn, our philosophy of life as embedded in our documents—the Declaration of Independence and the Constitution. Just the concept of "due process" alone would account for a great deal of litigation and case law that defines what administrators, teachers, and students can do in public education.

Bill Streshly and Larry Frase are both former school superintendents turned professors at San Diego State University. They approach their topic with the immediacy of having recently left the position of the chief executive officer, so the battles and scars are quite fresh. This compelling context has enabled them to develop a book that contains most of the common areas involving the law and derivative practices as they affect administrative practice in public schools.

I am sure readers of Streshly and Frase's small but significant book will come to appreciate their insights and conciseness in collecting the content of this text.

FENWICK W. ENGLISH
University of Kentucky

Preface

The purpose of this book is to provide busy school administrators with a quick source of information about the laws and court decisions that shape the playing field we call education. There are many fine, well-researched textbooks on U.S. public school law. As authors of this book, we do not intend to add another textbook to the list. Rather, this book is an executive summary of the legal issues and problems that face practicing school administrators. Only the more important cases are cited, and only the more critical legal principles are discussed. The book will serve to refresh the memory of the experienced, well-trained administrator, or it will serve as an orientation for the novice who wants a clear look at the big picture before delving into other specialized areas.

The book is both comprehensive and brief. It is comprehensive because it covers virtually every legal challenge faced by schools today. It is brief because the issues are summarized, emphasizing only the most important concepts.

Although the book has been reviewed by school attorneys for accuracy, we are not attorneys. We are experienced school administrators who have a combined administrative experience of

40 years in three different states. Our experience includes administration at all grade levels and virtually all positions from vice principal to superintendent. Consequently, discussions of legal principles are presented from the practitioner's perspective. In every chapter, an attempt has been made to merge the legal concerns of attorneys with the educational concerns of the practicing administrator.

Chapter 1 explains the governance of public education in America. The focus is upon the role of local school boards. Frequently encountered problems involving conflict of interest, closed sessions, and board policies are discussed from the standpoint of avoiding trouble.

Chapter 2 outlines the major legal issues facing schools today. The discussion emphasizes the broad drift of constitutional law in three critical areas: equality of opportunity, human rights, and separation of church and state. Practical examples provide guidelines for administrators concerning various aspects of equal access and student rights. The chapter concludes with a brief outline of the U.S. court system.

Chapters 3, 4, and 5 focus on the legal underpinnings of sound student management. Brief explanations of legal principles are followed by practical examples and advice. Chapter 3 deals with the management of instruction. Chapter 4 and Chapter 5 deal with planning for good school discipline and maintaining a safe campus.

The question of equal access for handicapped students has in recent years become one of the top three reasons to sue a school district. For this reason, Chapter 6 is devoted to the laws related to special education with a special emphasis on identification, placement, and appeal processes.

Chapter 7 offers advice to administrators in coping with the various legal problems of personnel management. The discussion outlines the problems and offers checklists of advice to avoid trouble.

The legal foundations of collective bargaining and the traditional processes are defined and discussed in Chapter 8. The discussion focuses on practical tips for contract management and suggests more productive models for employer-employee relations that might be pursued when the employees and the management of a district are ready.

Chapter 9 emphasizes risk management and program planning with the courts in mind. The chapter summarizes major planning strategies discussed in the previous eight chapters and emphasizes the need for proactive risk management in the school districts.

The Troubleshooting Guide provides an outline of critical legal problems and refers to pages in the book containing the solutions.

Special gratitude and appreciation are extended to Attorney Sandra Woliver for her review and criticism of the text. Ms. Woliver specializes in school law with the firm of Lozano, Smith, Smith, Woliver and Behrens of San Rafael, California. Special thanks are also in order for graduate students Rick Montgomery from Calgary, Alberta, and Faye Cabral and Josie Wilson from Edmonton, Alberta, for their contributions of library research.

WILLIAM A. STRESHLY
LARRY E. FRASE
San Diego State University

NOTES

About the Authors

William A. Streshly is Associate Professor of Administration, Rehabilitation, and Post-Secondary Education at San Diego State University. He has 25 years of experience in public school administration, including more than 13 years as district superintendent, 5 years as high school principal, 5 years as vice principal, and 2 years as counselor and student activities adviser. Currently, he teaches school law and finance in addition to coordinating San Diego State University's Administrative Credential Program. He has published articles on character education, staff development, curriculum development, competency testing, school finance, school labor relations, restructuring schools, and managing change. He has served as speaker and consultant for more than 30 state and national conferences, school districts, and professional organizations, in addition to scores of speaking engagements for community service clubs, chambers of commerce, alumni clubs, and political groups. He has served as a leader in numerous community/civic organizations and has served as an educational adviser to county, state, and federal officials.

Larry E. Frase is Professor of Organizational Psychology at San Diego State University. He has 16 years of experience in school administration, including 6 years as assistant superintendent and 8 as superintendent. He completed his M.A. and his Ph.D. at Arizona State University. He has published 40 articles in state and national journals and is currently working on articles ranging from school board reform to teacher motivation. *School Management by Wandering Around* (1990) is being used in graduate courses and by practicing school administrators. His latest book is an anthology, *Motivating and Compensating Teachers* (1992). He has served as a speaker and/or consultant for more than 75 state and national conferences, school districts, and universities. He has received numerous honors and awards at professional conferences. He was selected as one of the Top One Hundred School Administrators in the United States in 1985 by the National School Board Association and the American Association of School Administrators.

1

Education's Legal Framework

1.1 Making the System Work for You

Knowing the legal system is essential for today's school executive. As our society becomes more educated and affluent, it also seems to become more litigious. The schools have increasingly become the targets of this litigation. School administrators have no choice; they must face this reality and embrace strategies to cope with it. This means keeping abreast of court decisions and legislation. It also means making awareness of the law an integral part of the school's operations, staff development, and curriculum development. This chapter outlines the legal frameworks of public schools at the federal, state, and local levels.

1.2 Free Public Education: An American Ideal

The idea of free public education first gained popularity in eighteenth-century America. The colonists linked education to the freedom and democracy they had just won from Mother England. The states gradually enacted tax laws to support free "common schools."

It was from this crucible that the American tradition of education was forged. American school systems, American governmental institutions, and the laws that shape them are inexorably bound by this common heritage.

1.3 The Role of the Federal Government

The Tenth Amendment to the Constitution of the United States reserves for the states "the powers not delegated to the federal government." Because education is not mentioned in the Constitution, it is presumed to be a state function. Consequently, school systems have developed as agencies of the state with the federal government playing a supportive role. Although the states operate their schools with little control exerted from Washington, the enactment of major federal aid to education programs has led to a dependence on federal funding. This dependence in recent years has increased Washington's influence over school districts. The threat of withdrawing funds is enough to force compliance with most federal regulations.

1.4 The Role of State Government

Contrary to popular belief, school districts are state institutions, not local ones. Most state legislatures have chosen to establish local agencies or school districts to carry out their constitutional mandates to provide public schools. These quasi-municipal corporations are similar in operation to the boards and councils that govern cities and special districts. This gives rise to the mistaken belief that the school district is simply another special district. Generally speaking, local special districts have jurisdiction over their assigned responsibilities. Unless the legislature grants it, however, local agencies, such as cities, water districts, and counties, have no authority over school districts. For example, school districts are usually not required to comply with local zoning regulations and building codes. The legislature in California, however, has ordered its educational agencies to obey local zoning ordinances when using land for other purposes than schools or instructional programs.

Parents and even board members are often surprised to learn that their school district is an arm of the state government and that board members are state officers. The courts, however, have long recognized the status of school boards and went a step further in 1943 when the U.S. Supreme Court declared that the Fourteenth Amendment protects students against creatures of the state—"boards of education not excepted" (*West Virginia State Board of Education v. Barnett,* 1943).

1.5 State Office of Education

Although the basic delivery system for education in the United States is the local school district, all 50 states have established a state office of education. The state-level administrative agencies are organized primarily to provide leadership for the districts. The vast majority of the states use a tripartite scheme composed of a superintendent or commissioner, a board or commission, and a state department of education. The state superintendent, who may be elected by the people at large or appointed by the state board, serves as the chief executive of the state department of education. Although most laws concerning education passed by the legislature are aimed directly at the local school boards, the state superintendent and state board are often given specific leadership roles to perform, such as developing guidelines, rules, and regulations. They are also charged with monitoring compliance with the laws and settling certain local controversies and conflicts. The administrative offices of the state usually have little direct line authority over school districts. Nevertheless, considerable pressure can be applied by threatening to withhold funds. Because most districts rely heavily upon state funding, the threat is all that is needed to enforce compliance.

1.6 The Role of the Intermediate Education Agencies

In most states, the intermediate education agency is the county board of education. A few states are divided into service regions. Years ago, these offices provided vital services and communication for small rural districts in the farmlands throughout our states. The county office provided critical support ranging from curriculum development and supervision to the certification of teachers. Today's sophisticated communication has significantly reduced the need for the intermediate level. Today, they serve as appeals boards for student transfers and expulsions, approve district boundaries, and provide assorted financial and operational services offered to districts on a contract basis.

1.7 The Role of Local School Boards

Local management of the schools is a uniquely American tradition. Unfortunately, this is frequently termed local *control,* a misnomer that causes more than its share of confusion. Local school boards are administrative agencies; that is, they carry out administrative functions delegated to them by the state legislature. *School boards cannot be granted legislative powers of a plenary nature. Hence no real control is possible—at least in terms of self-determination.* The U.S. Supreme Court sets the standard this way: A legislature may delegate legislative power to the school board only if it also describes what job must be done, who must do it, and what might be the scope of that person's authority (*Bowles v. Willingham,* 1944).

A. *The Functions of the School Boards*

As far as the law is concerned, administrative functions of school boards fall into two categories: ministerial and discretionary. Ministerial functions are those duties that must be performed by the board and its school district precisely as ordered in the law. Examples of ministerial functions delegated in law to the school board by the legislature include minimum graduation requirements, minimum number of minutes and days school is to be in session, sundry prohibitions of subject matter, and so on. In each case, school boards are required to adopt graduation requirements reflecting the state's minimum criteria, establish a school year in conformance with the state's minimum criteria, and so forth.

On the other hand, discretionary functions delegated to the school board allow board members considerable latitude to exercise judgment. Examples of this are hiring personnel, approving bills, and adopting textbooks. In exercising these discretionary powers, the school board is limited only by the requirements and the restrictions set forth in the statutes or in the state's constitution.

B. *Delegation of Authority*

School boards are allowed to delegate to administrators and staff the ministerial functions. For example, the school board, after establishing graduation requirements, allows the administration to determine who graduates and who does not. Likewise, administrators organize the daily schedules and manage the instructional program. Discretionary functions, on the other hand, cannot be delegated. Only the board hires, approves bills, and adopts textbooks, for example.

Generally speaking, the courts are not inclined to interfere with the school board's exercise of discretion, even when it appears to be unwise. The exception to this, of course, is when the board's actions run afoul of the constitution or some other state law. Also, the courts may intervene in rare instances when the board appears to be abusing its authority or acting beyond its authority. The key to surviving court review of administrator or school board actions seems to be "reasonableness." This concept will be discussed further in ensuing chapters.

c. Limitations on School Board Membership

School board members are not permitted to hold another public office if the two offices are incompatible. The problem, of course, is determining whether or not a conflict exists. Generally, if the offices are both located in the governance hierarchy of education, they are considered to be in conflict. It is clear that membership on the county board of education would be in conflict with membership on a local district board. It is not clear, however, whether city council membership is in conflict with school board membership, unless, of course, the school board is appointed by the city council.

It has been an established principle in law that employees of a school district are not eligible for membership on its governing board unless they resign their positions. A recent lower court decision in California threatens to revise this principle. A school district employee ran for the board, won, and was allowed to take office by the superior court. An appeal is pending.

Individual school board members only have authority during board meetings unless delegated to act by board action. This is an important concept for administrators and teachers to understand, especially during an era when board members frequently decide to do freelance investigations of the school district. Unauthorized individual board members are *not* permitted to examine the students' cumulative files, nor are they entitled to review confidential employee records. Only when the board, in a legally constituted meeting, directs the staff to bring the records forth are the individual members permitted to examine these confidential records. One superintendent periodically reminds his staff that they should deal with board members as they do with their PTA presidents. In other words, treat them as special, influential, and very interested members of the community. But, just as administrators would not allow the PTA president to rifle through the cumulative files, they must not allow individual board members to violate student privacy and records laws.

D. *School Board Minutes*

A board speaks through its actions and minutes and only then when the action is prescribed by a motion and passed by the majority of a quorum. Comments by individual board members really only have historical value. All states have laws requiring boards to take minutes and store them as official records of the district.

E. *Board Member Conflict of Interest*

Nearly all states have statutes that prevent their public officers from having an interest in contracts made with the agencies they administer. Most states have gone a step further and adopted elaborate disclosure processes as additional safeguards. The term *interest* includes more than ownership. In West Virginia, the supreme court ordered the removal of board members from office after they had knowingly approved payments to their employer, a local contractor (*West v. Jones*, 1984). In Virginia, the courts prevented a city councilman from voting on appointments to the school board in the district in which he was employed (*Summers County Citizens League v. Tassos*, 1988).

F. *Removal From Office*

School board members may be removed from office for cause, such as the misconduct demonstrated by the West Virginia school board members by contracting with their employers. Cause for removal from office includes malfeasance, improper or illegal performance of duties, breach of good faith, or inefficiency and incapacity. The courts, however, are reluctant to remove politicians from office for anything short of blatant criminal misconduct. The most common remedy used by the citizenry to oust incapable or unpopular politicians is the recall election. In most states, a simple petition process will result in a recall election to decide whether the targeted politicians will keep their elected offices.

G. *Controlling Board Member Conduct*

School boards often adopt bylaws concerning the conduct of their membership. Because these bylaws cannot modify or conflict with state statutes and constitutions, they tend to be guidelines rather than strict regulations. School boards, however, have used these bylaws effectively to censure errant members. Because board members occupy politically sensitive positions, pressure of this sort, generated through board self-regulation, often is effective.

H. *School Board's Voting*

In the absence of statutes providing otherwise, a school board quorum is a simple majority of the board. Some states, such as California, require a vote of a majority of the total number of board members. Usually school boards adopt Robert's Rules of Order to govern the conduct of meetings. By reference, these rules are adopted in a bylaw and become a legal part of the process to fulfill board obligations. When school boards fail to strictly observe their own duly adopted bylaws concerning meeting procedures, they take the chance of having their actions nullified by the court.

I. *School Board Meetings*

Board members carry out their official functions as board members only at school board meetings, and school board meetings occur only when they are properly noticed and convened in strict conformance with the directives of the state statutes. These directives usually require the following:

- The agenda must be posted in certain specified public places 24 to 72 hours before the meeting.
- The media must be notified.
- The date, time, and location must be clearly announced.
- The agenda for the meeting must be listed. Several states require that the agenda be described in enough detail that the public will be able to understand what action is being contemplated and which organizations, companies, or people are involved.
- Executive or closed sessions should be announced along with the topics to be discussed in the closed session.

Failure to properly notify the public of a school board meeting means that it is not a meeting as such. Consequently, board members have no authority to act. Any actions taken by the board during an improperly noticed meeting may be declared void. It is not hard to imagine the complications that can occur as the result of an administrator's failing to properly post notice of a meeting. The rules are simple but should be kept handy for ready reference to avoid the political and legal entanglements of a slipup.

J. Executive Sessions or Closed Meetings

A growing number of states have enacted so-called open meeting laws. Most of these laws are a result of the efforts by newspaper lobbies to promote "the public's right to know." The laws require that school boards conduct all of their business in public, including the conversations and discussions leading up to the public board action. Generally, it is considered a violation of these laws if a quorum of the board meets informally to discuss school matters. It is not an infraction for one board member to discuss school matters with another board member outside a legally constituted meeting unless other board members constituting a majority of the board are also present. The courts have further ruled that attempts to circumvent the letter of the law by gathering consensus through a chain of phone calls or other devious methods are illegal acts and constitute misconduct on the part of the board members involved.

The open meeting laws allow the board to close its doors and meet out of the view of the public (and the press) for certain specified reasons. Usually these include the following:

Instructing the board's negotiator in the collective bargaining process.

Discussing matters relating to employee discipline, student discipline, and other personal matters protected by privacy laws. This does *not* mean that the board may meet behind closed doors and talk about personnel or students *in general*. Rather, only specific individuals may be discussed under this exception. For example, it is illegal to discuss, in closed session, the possible elimination of counselor positions at the high schools; however, meeting to discuss whether or not to initiate disciplinary action against a specific counselor is legal under the law.

Consulting with the board's attorney concerning pending or threatened litigation. Some attorneys believe that the key in this exception is the presence of the attorney. Others feel that it is appropriate for the superintendent to relay letters and messages from the attorney and to gather reactions and directions to be relayed to the attorney. In any event, the board should rely upon the guidance of its attorney relative to the use of this exception.

Discussing the negotiations to purchase real property (land or buildings). This exception is similar to the one for instructing the labor negotiator. It is not in the public's interest to force the custodians of its tax dollars to tip their hands in public meetings by disclosing bid strategies.

Dealing with matters of security such as undercover police investigations and other actions to protect the students and the interests of the district.

Open meeting laws also apply to various other groups appointed by the school board to carry out its ministerial duties or to gather data and make recommendations. The key here is that the discussion leading up to the recommendation is part of the decision. Because the discussion is being carried on by a duly appointed board committee, it is subject to the open meeting rules. State statutes vary, but in some cases a special citizens' committee, appointed by the board to make recommendations to the board, also must comply with all of the agenda posting and meeting laws, including notification of the newspapers.

K. *Board Elections*

Methods for electing or appointing school board members vary from state to state. Most states simply prescribe election of board members on one of the state's regular election days. In many large cities, the city council or mayor appoints the school board. In the South, a few self-perpetuating school boards who appoint their own members still exist. In Washington, DC, Delaware, and Pennsylvania, judges appoint the board members. For obvious reasons, the rules and regulations for being elected to the school board must be strictly observed by the candidates. Because most school board candidates are relative novices politically, the burden of informing board members and candidates of the various and sometimes intricate rules and regulations falls on the school administrator.

Administrators also need to be aware of one-person/one-vote laws, especially when drawing precincts within the district for trustee representation and residency requirements. In Alabama, an appeals court reacted to a Voting Rights Act violation by taking matters into its own hands and prescribing a school district's voting areas (*U.S. v. Dallas County Common,* 1988).

L. *Board Policies*

In theory, boards establish policies, then hire administrators to carry them out. The board's function from this point forward is to sit in judgment on various policy infractions and the quality of administrator performance. Needless to say, the process is not as simple as it sounds. Modern-day board members often want to get far more involved in the day-to-day administration of the district, inevitably causing headaches for the administration.

M. *Board-Administration Relations*

The courts have recognized, though, that the unique nature of a school board's mission makes it impossible to remain completely objective in all matters. The mixture of executive, legislative, and judicial functions requires that courts grant latitude to boards to function in various roles. In Wisconsin, for example, the teachers association sued the board when the board fired members of the faculty in the district for going on strike—an exercise of its "judicial" function. The teachers argued that the circumstances were not conducive to "detachment and impartiality" on the part of the school board. The U.S. Supreme Court did not agree, declaring "mere familiarity with the facts of the case gained by an agency in the performance of its statutory role does not . . . disqualify a decision maker" (*Hortonville J.S.D. v. Hortonville Education Association,* 1975).

The key to avoiding these problems is to develop a clear understanding of board and administrator roles. Particularly effective techniques used by superintendents to accomplish these worthy goals include the following:

- Conduct board workshops and new board member workshops focusing on the organizational rationale for carefully defining and separating roles. The emphasis here is on a smartly designed management scheme.
- Adopt board policies and bylaws that formally outline the roles for trustees and administrators governing the district.
- Install a precision system for developing, distributing, and enforcing administrative procedures to carry out board policy. The emphasis here is on providing an administrative system that deals adequately with various contingencies. In other words, this leaves no room for adventuresome trustees to claim that there is no means for responding to legitimate claims of their constituents.

TABLE 1.1 Federal and State Court Systems

Level	Federal Court System	Typical State Court System
Highest	U.S. Supreme Court	State Supreme Court
Appeals	Federal Court of Appeals	State Appellate Court
Trial	Federal District Court	State District Court (or Superior Court)

1.8 The Judicial System

Before the adoption of our Constitution, each of the original 13 colonies had its own judicial system. This caused major problems as there was no system for dealing with disputes between the states or for handling citizens convicted by a court in another state. The designers of our Constitution solved the problem by establishing a federal court system. It is interesting that they left the state and local systems intact, creating the unique U.S. dual court system. Table 1.1 describes the federal court system and a typical state court system.

A. The State Court System

At the bottom of the state systems are the municipal courts and justice courts. These usually handle only misdemeanors, minor crimes, and civil cases involving a certain monetary limit. Litigation of a more serious nature begins at the next level, the superior court. Trials are conducted at both the municipal and the superior court levels.

B. Appeal of Superior Court Decisions

In most states, an appeal of a superior court decision is made to the court of appeals, whose function is to review the decisions of the lower court and to ensure fair and consistent application of the law. The appeals court rarely hears new evidence. Its purpose is to check for errors in procedure or misinterpretation of the law by the lower court. If an error or misinterpretation is spotted, the court either reverses the decision or sends it back to the lower court with orders to repair the damage.

c. *The State Supreme Court*

The highest court in most state court systems is the state supreme court. The court performs essentially the same function as the court of appeals. Its decisions are final, unless, of course, questions of federal law are involved. In these cases, appeals from a state supreme court go directly to the U.S. Supreme Court.

d. *The Federal Court System*

In the federal system, the lowest courts of original jurisdiction are the federal district courts, and their jurisdiction is over federal law. The district court is the trial court in the federal system. Appeals from the district courts are made to the federal circuit courts of appeals. The entire process is very similar to the appeals to the appellate courts from the superior courts in the state system, except that the questions involved concern federal law instead of state law. The highest court of appeals in the United States is, of course, the U.S. Supreme Court. Although its primary function is to review decisions of lower courts, in rare instances of dissention between states and the federal government, the Supreme Court acts as the court of original jurisdiction.

e. *The Dual Court System*

The dual court system hierarchy described above is more or less in place in every state of the Union with a few exceptions. For instance, some states do not have courts of appeals; instead, decisions are appealed directly to the state's supreme court. In other states, the *highest* court is called the Court of Appeals and, in the State of New York, the lower trial court is called the Supreme Court and the highest court is the Court of Appeals. The names notwithstanding, the structures are very similar.

Appeals to the appellate court (court of appeals) from the superior court (or district court) are heard as a matter of routine, providing there is even the slightest basis for an appeal. The appellate court will review the case, hear arguments concerning errors in procedure or misinterpretation of law, and render a decision accordingly.

The supreme courts, on the other hand, sift through the cases appealed to them and accept only those that seem to have unique circumstances needing interpretation of the law. Usually the briefs presented to the supreme courts are reviewed by all the justices and, if a certain number of them feel the case has merit, it is heard by the court. Otherwise, it is simply rejected and the appellate court decision stands.

1.9 Keeping Abreast of the Law in Education

Through continuing litigation at all levels in hundreds of courts throughout our nation, the laws affecting education are shaped and reshaped. School administrators recognize that less energy (and certainly less money) is consumed if the school system is able to anticipate legal trends. Then administrators can shape their organizations to conform to the new legal requirements. Staying abreast of the law is one of the newer but more essential challenges facing the administrator. The key is to keep abreast of what's happening in the lower courts. Waiting until a supreme court decision is made may be expensive in terms of time, energy, and resources. Keeping up is really not hard. Legal briefings are a regular feature of many commercial journals and publications. For instance, Perry Zirkel runs a very informative column at the end of the *Phi Delta Kappan* each month, titled "De Jure." The more serious school administrator can subscribe to one of the several school law newsletters, which are very complete and authoritative.

Finally, most of the local state and federal administrator associations and school board associations include legal briefings on current issues as featured sections in their seasonal conventions. Modern school administrators would be well advised to include these features of the conventions in their agenda.

Key Terms

❑ *Agenda*. A description of items to be discussed at a board meeting, which must be publicly posted usually 24 to 72 hours before a meeting.

❑ *Appellate court*. A panel of judges that hears appeals from lower courts.

❑ *Board bylaws*. A series of board policies specifying the rules for conduct of meetings and the conduct of board members.

❑ *Board meetings*. A legally advertised meeting of a quorum of the board members.

❑ *Boardsmanship*. A board member's skill and knowledge relating to the protocols required to properly manage a school organization.

❑ *Circuit court of appeals*. A federal appeals court that hears cases from lower federal courts.

❑ *Cumulative file*. The school's file used to collect a student's records.

❑ *Executive session or closed session*. A private meeting of the board wherein only certain matters specified by law may be discussed.

❑ *Federal district court*. A lower (trial) court in the federal court system.

❑ *Free public education*. The ideal of providing a free common education to all citizens; a concept that first became popular in the United States after the American Revolution.

❑ *Intermediate educational agencies (also known as county offices of education and regional offices of education)*. An administrative agency providing regional support and services for local school districts.

❑ *Local control*. The degree of discretion and authority granted by the legislature to the school boards to operate the local schools.

❑ *Local school boards*. A local committee, usually elected, charged with the responsibility of operating schools according to the guidelines established by the legislature.

❑ *Ministerial and discretionary functions*. Ministerial functions are carefully prescribed by law and allow no modification at the local level; discretionary functions specify local options or decisions.

❏ *Municipal court or justice of the peace.* A lower court in the state system.

❏ *Plenary power.* Power of a complete nature. Local school boards do not have plenary power; the legislature does.

❏ *Recall election.* A special election held to oust incumbent politicians during their terms; the election is the result of a petition as specified by law.

❏ *State commission or board of education.* A state-level committee usually appointed by the governor; each committee carries out various policymaking and administrative duties assigned by the legislature.

❏ *State court system.* A system of courts, separate from the federal courts, that deals primarily with matters of state law.

❏ *State office of education.* The chief educational administrative agency for a state.

❏ *State superintendent or commissioner of public instruction.* The state's chief educational official; carries out functions as directed by the legislature and the state constitution.

❏ *State supreme court.* The highest court in the state court system.

❏ *Superior court.* A lower (trial) court in the state system.

❏ *Tenth Amendment.* An amendment to the U.S. Constitution that reserves to the states powers not delegated to the federal government; education is a state function because it is not mentioned in the Constitution.

❏ *U.S. Supreme Court.* The highest court of the land.

References

Bowles v. Willingham, 321 U.S. 503 64 S.Ct. 641 (1944).

Hortonville J.S.D. v. Hortonville Education Association, 225 N.W.2d 658 (Wis. 1975).

Summers County Citizens League v. Tassos, 367 S.E.2d 209 (W.Va. 1988).

U.S. v. Dallas County Common, Dallas County Ala., 850 F.2d 1422 (11th Cir. 1988).

West v. Jones, 323 S.E.2d 96 (Va. 1984).

West Virginia State Board of Education v. Barnett, 319 U.S. 624 (1943).

2

Coping With the Major Issues

2.1 Understanding the Direction of the Changing Law

It is worth repeating: Today's school administrator must keep track of the shifting legal sands underpinning our school systems. Understanding the direction of the law gives the administrator the ability to anticipate changes needed to conform and to avoid unnecessary and debilitating litigation. Having said that, it is necessary to point out that broad historical trends must be understood in order to grasp the significance of recent developments. Several dominant issues have affected the court decisions, muddling America's public schools during the past 50 years. They have caused substantial change and, in some cases, unnecessary confusion among school administrators. These dominant issues can be broadly categorized into three groups:

- the search for equality and problems with discrimination,
- the struggle for human rights, and
- the separation of church and state.

Understanding these issues is really a matter of understanding where this nation has been and where it is going. From this perspective alone can the educator make sense of it all.

2.2 The Search for Equality

A. *Separate but Equal Overturned*

In 1954, the *Brown v. Board of Education* case kicked off nearly four decades of litigation affecting virtually every aspect of the nation's public school operations. The U.S. Supreme Court reversed the half-century old doctrine of "separate but equal." For the first half of the twentieth century, the Court had supported state laws in the South calling for separate facilities for blacks and whites. In the *Plessy v. Ferguson* (1896) case, the Court ruled that Louisiana law could prohibit a man who was one-eighth black and seven-eighths white from sitting in the "white" section of a train, so long as the "black" facilities were essentially equal. Consequently, until 1954, "separate but equal" restaurants, barber shops, rest rooms, and, of course, schools continued to flourish.

In the *Brown* case (1954), the Court examined the psychological effects of segregation on black children. The Court found segregated schools to be "inherently unequal" and consequently a violation of the Equal Protection Clause of the Fourteenth Amendment.

The *Brown* case gave birth to a major movement in the public schools. Although Brown at first seemed to apply only to school facilities of black children in the South, the notion that the Fourteenth Amendment guaranteed equal access to public facilities was firmly established across the nation. It would also soon affect other aspects of school operations.

B. *Racial Discrimination*

In 1975, the Supreme Court strongly affirmed the broad discretionary powers of the federal courts to implement desegregation plans, including court-ordered bussing (*Swann v. Charlotte*, 1970). In addition, the principles of desegregation had been expanded to include integration of faculties (*Rogers v. Paul*, 1965). School executives struggled with new affirmative action plans. These included quotas, which specified that a certain ratio of minority groups must be represented on the faculty. The black former superintendent of public instruction in California, Wilson Riles, was fond of criticizing racial quotas in the classroom as a means for creating excellence. Citing his state's growing minority population, he would chide largely white administrator audiences by pointing out, "Soon there will not be enough of you to go around." Dr. Riles's comment, made during the late 1970s, served to remind California administrators of the central purpose of the desegregation efforts, namely, equal access to high-quality education. The *Brown* case mandated desegregation to assure equal access to the wealth and resources of the state as guaranteed by the Fourteenth Amendment. In subsequent decisions, the Court has reaffirmed its support of desegregation, but it has stopped short of defining racial balance as the goal.

The principles of equal protection guaranteed by the Fourteenth Amendment and revisited in the *Brown* case became part of the core of the U.S. civil rights movement. In 1964, Congress passed the Civil Rights Act, which further elaborated upon the Fourteenth Amendment's equal protection principles by declaring that no person "shall on the grounds of race, color or national origin . . . be subject to discrimination under any program receiving federal financial assistance."

C. *Handicap Discrimination*

In the spirit of *Brown,* the concept of equal access to public schools was expanded to include handicapped children. In 1971, a federal court ruled that mentally retarded children must be educated in regular classrooms whenever possible (*Pennsylvania Association for Retarded Children v. Commonwealth*, 1971). Soon, other similar cases were initiated with similar outcomes. The lower courts constantly reinforced the principle that all children were entitled to an appropriate free education, and "separate but equal" facilities would not always pass constitutional muster. In one case, the court ordered the school district to provide "individualized educational plans" and "due process" procedures (*Mills v. Bd of Education*, 1972).

D. *Individuals With Disabilities Education Act*

The question of whether the Fourteenth Amendment guarantees access for the handicapped to public schools never reached the Supreme Court during these early years. In 1973, Congress passed the Vocational Rehabilitation Act and, in 1975, the Education for All Handicapped Children Act (Public Law 94-142).

The Vocational Rehabilitation Act outlawed discrimination of the handicapped under any program or activity receiving federal financial assistance. It also required that new public facilities be built to allow access by the handicapped.

The Education for All Handicapped Children Act (now the Individuals with Disabilities Education Act, or IDEA) clarified some of the language found in earlier federal court cases. It required schools to provide "individualized educational plans" and "due process" in addition to a "free appropriate education" in the "least restrictive learning environment"—phrases that have become commonplace in the vocabulary of today's educators across the nation. These topics are discussed further in Chapter 6.

E. *Gender Discrimination*

In 1972, Congress again preempted Supreme Court action and outlawed sex discrimination in the schools. Title IX of the Education Amendments of 1972 (PL 92-318) forbids schools to conduct programs that subject their students to discrimination on the basis of gender. Prior to 1972, most school administrators were anticipating a law or ruling of this sort and had begun opening educational opportunities for female students and working to eliminate stereotypes. In reality, Title IX merely applied specifically to schools what the Civil Rights Act of 1964 applied generally to U.S. society.

Twenty years after the passage of Title IX of the Education Amendments, de facto gender discrimination remains pervasive, especially in U.S. high schools. For example, certain classes such as auto mechanics and woodworking are almost exclusively male, while business skills and "food science" (the modern euphemism for *homemaking*) are primarily female.

Most of the lawsuits in this area have been focused on athletic programs. In general, the courts have ruled that females may compete with males in noncontact sports, providing the school offers no comparable sports setting for females.

Participation in contact sports is another question. Some courts seem to recognize that segregated programs make sense based on the physical differences between boys and girls, so long as the girls have a comparable program. Other courts have struck down the rules preventing girls from participating in contact sports reserved for boys even if a comparable program exists (*Yellowsprings Exempted Village School District Board of Education v. Ohio School Athletic Association*, 1978). These decisions are based on the unequivocal language of Title IX and the Fourteenth Amendment. After all, separate *is* inherently unequal.

Sooner or later, one of these cases will find its way to the Supreme Court and the ground rules will be clarified. To date, the Court has been reluctant to strike down gender-based classifications if they have a reasonable, rational basis.

An interesting variation of this issue confronted a California school superintendent during the 1984 Olympic games. The performance of the U.S. men's volleyball team prompted several of the boys in the area high schools to "demand" that they be allowed to join the girls' volleyball teams and compete. At that time, there were no male volleyball teams competing in the area high schools. The girls' volleyball team was matched with the boys' football team to provide the "comparable" sports setting. The superintendent upheld the ban on male participation and was subsequently scolded by the students for reverse discrimination. The matter never reached the lawsuit stage (a rumor that the boys had been beaten by the girls' volleyball team was never substantiated).

F. *Language Discrimination*

In the mid-1970s, the Supreme Court ruled that a school district's failure to accommodate the special needs of non-English-speaking students violated the Civil Rights Act of 1964, in particular the section that prohibits discrimination based on "race, color, or *national origin*." At first, the ruling was interpreted as a mandate that teachers throughout the system teach non-English-speaking students in their native languages. This caused widespread concern among many educators, especially in the areas of the country heavily affected by immigrants. In California, for instance, it is not uncommon for a single student body to have 30 or more primary languages represented. Although the Court did not define the school districts' responsibilities in detail, it emphasized that students who do not understand English are effectively deprived of their right to a meaningful education.

School districts that have been successful in meeting the needs of non-English- and limited-English-speaking students have found the key to be a strong acceptance among all staff of the concept enunciated by the Supreme Court. This is the idea that the mission of public schools is not only to educate the masses but also to serve as a social escalator, which is a primary instrument of the American ideal of equal opportunity. These districts have developed sophisticated plans that include staff development, curriculum development, parent education, and teacher recruitment.

G. *Socioeconomic Discrimination*

Rendering the schools accessible to all of America's children has been a laudable goal of the Supreme Court and Congress. The attempt to remove the barriers of discrimination for race, sex, handicap, and language have been relatively successful. Modern educators, however, recognize that a major barrier to equal access to a high-quality education by all American children is *poverty.* This affects the public schools in two ways: First, the disadvantaged or poor families come to school equipped with "major" physical and psychological barriers to learning. Second, the schools in the neighborhoods where these children reside are often underfunded, neglected, or both.

The Elementary and Secondary Education Act. In 1965, Congress passed the massive Elementary and Secondary Education Act as part of President Johnson's War on Poverty. This resulted in the largest federal aid to education in the nation's history. Compensatory Education or Title I (now known as Chapter 1) infused massive federal dollars into schools with high concentrations of students with families on welfare. Since then, other programs such as the preschool Headstart program and the free lunch program have been added to help eliminate the barriers to education created by poverty. Many of the states have opted to join with the federal government's effort by contributing additional state dollars to the compensatory education programs.

But even massive federal programs such as the Elementary and Secondary Education Act were unable to compensate for the huge inequities in funding created by the property taxation method of funding schools. This method, which was widespread throughout the United States until the mid-1970s, caused schools in high-wealth areas to be well funded and capable of a rich variety of educational and cultural programs for their children. Schools in low-wealth districts, on the other hand, were poorly funded and incapable of offering a high-quality education.

Property tax inequity. In 1971, the California Supreme Court handed down the landmark *Serrano v. Priest* (1971) decision, which declared that the quality of a child's education should not be determined by the quality of the neighborhood in which he or she lives. In establishing the principle of "fiscal neutrality," the court ruled that the quality of California schools must be based on the wealth of the state as a whole, not the wealth of a local school district. The legislature was ordered to revise its school finance methods to provide for equal funding for all schools in the state.

Following the *Serrano* case in California, a rash of lawsuits in other states produced similar decisions from the state supreme courts. In 1973, students in San Antonio, Texas, filed a *Serrano*-type case in the federal court system hoping that the federal courts, and eventually the U.S. Supreme Court, would settle the matter once and for all. It is surprising that the Court ruled against the plaintiffs in this case (*San Antonio v. Rodriguez,* 1973) and declared that education was not a fundamental right explicitly protected by the Constitution. Because Texas had not deprived the students of due process or liberty or property, the Supreme Court would not intervene.

The U.S. Supreme Court ruling did not stop the cases from being heard in the various states one at a time, and in 1990 the Texas Supreme Court joined most of the other states in the Union in declaring its property tax-based school finance system unconstitutional.

H. *Ability Discrimination*

Dividing students into ability groups is a long-standing tradition in American education. In the last three decades, however, it has come under increasing attack. Detractors claim it often results in racial or cultural segregation. Others argue that the impact of ability segregation upon the student is as damaging as racial or gender segregation. Generally, however, the question is more professional than legal unless a grouping practice can be shown to be racially or culturally biased. Following this line of reasoning, the courts have struck down the use of norm-referenced intelligence tests for placing students. The court found that the cultural bias of these tests results in racial and cultural discrimination (*Larry P. v. Riles,* 1979). Where no segregation or discrimination results, the courts support the use of tests for student placement (*Smith v. Dallas County Bd of Education,* 1979). The key for administrators is to avoid tests that tend to identify students based on cultural or racial minority background.

An interesting side issue of the ability discrimination question is posed by the large number of male students segregated
into so-called educationally handicapped or learning handicapped classes. The criteria for placement in these classes is
often based on playground or classroom deportment. The
classes are normally 80% to 90% male students. The handicaps
are often related to "attention deficits" or "emotional problems."
As one school superintendent remarked, "If any race or ethnic
group were segregated by our placement practices as boy students are segregated, we would have a federal civil rights investigation on our hands."

I. Other Areas of Discrimination

Recently, questions of discrimination against homosexuals
have risen in several areas of the country. To the credit of school
administrators, most of these have not become court cases. As
long as the school administrations do not attempt to discrimi-
nate or classify students in a capricious or arbitrary manner,
the courts will support their authority to organize learning programs, including classifying students. For example, classifying
students by age has been supported by the courts (*Hammond v.
Marx,* 1975). The key is a reasonable and rational basis for the
regulation.

2.3 The Struggle for Human Rights:
Students, Parents

The 1960s and 1970s were decades of great change in our society. Nowhere was this more acute than on the campuses of our
public schools. A generation of students trying to express themselves ran headlong into a school system steeped in the tradition of *in loco parentis.* Acting in the place of parents, schools
exercised broad control over student behavior. Conscientious
staff felt justified in demanding that their students comply with
generally accepted protocols ranging from manners and morals
to dress and grooming. Heretofore, the courts had backed them

up, declaring that in the school, as in the family, "there exists on the part of the pupils the obligations of obedience to lawful commands, subordination, civil deportment." The courts, school administrators, and perhaps most of the American people in prior years had agreed that this teacher-pupil relationship was proper and was, in fact, a commonsensical "law" of school systems.

A. *Student Rights*

The *in loco parentis* bubble burst in 1969 with the landmark *Tinker v. Des Moines Independent School District* decision. The Court overruled a policy adopted by the principals of the Des Moines schools that forbid students from wearing black arm-bands protesting the Vietnam war. The arm-bands were judged to be a silent expression of an idea and, accordingly, protected by the First Amendment guaranteeing freedom of speech. The thrust of the impact of the Court's decision was felt throughout our school systems, as one by one the school dress and grooming codes were dropped. But the *Tinker* case had a more significant impact as a result of the language used by the Court to support its decision. Using powerful rhetoric, the Court declared, "It can hardly be argued that either students or teachers shed their Constitutional rights . . . at the schoolhouse gate." The notion that school officials can arbitrarily control student speech or grooming or dress was dead. Also dead was the notion that con-stitutional rights of any sort could be abridged by school officials for the purpose of "properly" conducting school. If the speech (or clothing) was clearly disruptive or dangerous to student wel-fare, it could be prohibited, but the "parental" attitude of pro-hibiting speech simply because it seems prudent to do so was no longer permitted in the schools.

In subsequent cases, the lower courts and the Supreme Court have reemphasized that the constitutional guarantees that stu-dents enjoy should not disrupt the orderly conduct of school. In appropriate situations, school administrators can take action to prevent gangs from wearing their colors or other special insig-nia on campus. Similarly, teachers and administrators can con-trol speech in classes and in student publications. The key words, which will be discussed in a later chapter, are *control* and *regulation,* not *prohibition.*

B. *Parent Rights*

In recent years, school administrators have been faced with a growing demand for so-called parent rights. These include matters ranging from inspecting a child's cumulative file to requesting that a child be excluded from instruction in conflict with family values. In California, for example, school administrators are required to notify parents of more than a dozen different "rights" prior to a student's enrollment in the school.

Although on the surface many of these rights seem reasonable, each of them is vulnerable to interpretation by various special interest groups who may not be reasonable. For example, the California prohibition on administering questionnaires that ask students about family matters was interpreted by one northern California family to mean an English teacher should be prohibited from asking his students to write about what their families did over the summer. Another religious group interpreted the parent right to inspect the family life curriculum to mean the group could enter classrooms to "preview" the lessons (and show disapproval) regardless of whether their children were enrolled in the class. Naturally, there is no shortage of attorneys who will vigorously prosecute these points of law.

C. *Teacher Rights*

At the beginning of this century, teachers in many areas were still being dismissed for unsatisfactory personal conduct including smoking, drinking alcoholic beverages, or marrying. In terms of full citizenship, teachers have come a long way since the turn of the century. But the struggle continues. Today's society continues to question the limits of the public school teacher's academic freedom and freedom of speech. After all, the public has entrusted its most precious possession, its children, to the care of school personnel. It is natural for the public to desire control over the character of the people employed. Administrators acting for the public have a duty to protect the children by dismissing personnel who would be dangerous or damaging to the children. Just as student conduct must be managed within the bounds of constitutionality, administrators also have a responsibility to establish staff regulations conducive to the proper conduct of school. Predictably, exercise of this responsibility has resulted in litigation on subjects ranging from dress codes to loyalty oaths to prayer in the classroom.

As it did for students, the Supreme Court has reaffirmed that teachers are "persons" and do not shed their constitutional rights at the schoolhouse gates. The special circumstances of the profession require that some rights be controlled and regulated. Again, the guiding principle is whether the behavior or actions are detrimental to the welfare of the general student body or to the conduct of schooling.

2.4 Separation of Church and State

Long held to be one of the basic tenets of our government, government officials have attempted to establish schools that do not embrace, adopt, promote, or conflict with established religion. In past years, this has meant the elimination of religiously oriented lessons in the classroom and prayers at school ceremonies. The courts seem to be moving in two different directions on this issue. The ban on religious prayer at school graduation ceremonies and religion-oriented programs in the classroom (for example, Christmas pageants and Christmas caroling) is gradually becoming stricter. This means that allowing Jewish children to describe their Hanukkah gifts no longer excuses a full-blown, three-week Christmas celebration in the classroom. On the other hand, the courts seem to be moving toward greater freedom of religious expression on the school grounds for students. A recent Supreme Court case affords First Amendment protection to religious discussion and prayer meetings on campuses so long as they are not sponsored by the school district (*Board of Education of West Side Community Schools District v. Mergens,* 1990; *West v. Jones,* 1984).

The support of church-run schools by tax dollars was also forbidden at one point in history. Since World War II, there has been an erosion of this principle. Returning GIs were supported by the GI Bill to attend the schools of their choices including religious schools. Later, the Court ruled that federal tax funds could be used by private and parochial schools to purchase textbooks—the key being that the dollars follow the students with special needs. Similarly, placement of children in church-sponsored, private schools and institutions, at taxpayer expense, has been supported when the public school systems could not accommodate the special needs of certain handicapped children. Most recently, the question of whether to allow educational vouchers to be spent at parochial schools as well as private and public schools is being debated. Because educational vouchers are not at all widespread in the United States, the discussions are not urgent. They do, however, tend to underscore this trend.

Key Terms

- ❑ *Civil Rights Act of 1964.* A law passed by Congress that further elaborated and expanded the Fourteenth Amendment's equal protection principles; violators would not be eligible for federal funds.

- ❑ *Compensatory Education (Chapter 1).* Program supported by funds allocated to schools to offset the social and educational impact of poverty.

- ❑ *Cultural bias.* The tendency for certain instruments (achievement tests, for example) to be more appropriate for use with students of one particular culture; tests used for grouping that result in racial segregation have been outlawed.

- ❑ *Desegregation.* The efforts to balance the racial makeup of school populations.

- ❑ *Due process.* The procedures that officials must observe before a right, such as education, can be modified or taken away from an individual as punishment.

- ❑ *Equal protection clause.* The clause of the Fourteenth Amendment that requires equal application of the laws to all persons in the United States.

- ❑ *IDEA (the Individuals with Disabilities Education Act; formerly the Education for all Handicapped Children's Act).* Guaranteed all handicapped children a "free appropriate education" in the "least restrictive learning environment."

❑ *Individualized educational plan.* The special plan for education worked out cooperatively with the school and the parents for the education of a handicapped child.

❑ *In loco parentis.* A legal principle that authorized school personnel to act in place of the parent.

❑ *Separate but equal.* Doctrine enunciated in the *Plessy v. Ferguson* (1896) case that allowed public facilities to be separated by race as long as they were "equal" in quality and quantity.

❑ *Title IX of the Education Amendments of 1972.* Outlawed discrimination on the basis of sex; violators would not be eligible for federal funds.

References

Board of Education of West Side Community Schools District v. Mergens, 110 S.Ct. 2356 (1990).

Brown v. Board of Education, 347 U.S. 483, 74 S.Ct. 686, 98 L.Ed. 873 (1954).

Hammond v. Marx, 406 F. Supp. 853 (D.Me. 1975).

Larry P. v. Riles, 495 F. Supp. 926 (D.C. Cal. 1979).

Mills v. Bd of Education, 348 F. Supp. 866 (D.D.C. 1972).

Pennsylvania Association for Retarded Children v. Commonwealth, 334 F. Supp. 1257 (E.D. Pa. 1971).

Plessy v. Ferguson, 163 U.S. 537, 16 S.Ct. 1138 (1896).

Rogers v. Paul, 382 U.S. 198, 86 S.Ct. 358, 15 L.Ed. 2d 265 (1965).

San Antonio I.S.D. v. Rodriguez, 411 U.S. 1 (1973).

Serrano v. Priest, 96 Cal. Rptr. 601 (1971).

Smith v. Dallas County Bd of Education, 480 F. Supp. 1324 (S.D. Ala 1979).

Swann v. Charlotte-Mecklenberg Board of Education, 402 U.S. 1, 91 S.Ct. 1267, 28 L.Ed. 2d 554 (1970).

Tinker v. Des Moines I.C.S.D., 393 U.S. 503, 89 S.Ct. 733, 21 L.Ed. 2d 731 (1969).

West v. Jones, 323 S.E.2d 96 (Va. 1984).

Yellowsprings Exempted Village School District Board of Education v. Ohio School Athletic Association, 443 F. Supp. 752 (S.D. Ohio 1978).

3

Laws Affecting Students

No one argues with President Kennedy's assertion that the goal of education is "the advancement of knowledge and the dissemination of truth." Whether or not that happens is the job of the schools' staff. That job is composed of thousands of delicate interpersonal relationships: smiles, exhortations, tears, encouragement. The business of school is human relations. Being sensitive and human may be the most important qualities of a principal, and a supportive climate, the most important attribute of a school. The school administrator is challenged with the task of simultaneously providing an environment that is safe and well disciplined yet supportive and nurturing. The two missions are not incompatible, but they represent the sort of complex human relations problem that can make or break a school.

The key to success depends on an awareness and understanding of the laws affecting students.

This chapter discusses key legal principles and traditional pitfalls important to school administration.

3.1 Compulsory Education: The Obligation and the Right to Attend Public Schools

The courts have long supported the notion that states have the legitimate power and authority to compel their children to attend school. Of more interest to the courts in recent years have been the questions of who will be excluded from public education and whether alternative forms of education such as home schooling comply with the compulsory education laws.

A. *The Rights of Married or Pregnant Students*

Until the late 1970s, students who were married or pregnant were routinely subject to special school rules. Often these rules involved placement in special schools or classes apart from the mainstream student body. The Civil Rights Act, Title IX, coupled with the Supreme Court's consistent interpretations of the Equal Protection Clause of the Fourteenth Amendment, have effectively outlawed discriminatory practices in schools based on marital status or pregnancy (*Davis v. Meek,* 1972). School-aged children who are married or pregnant are entitled to attend regular school without interruption. They cannot be compelled to attend, however, because of their special "emancipated" status.

B. *Undocumented Aliens*

The question of who must be afforded a public education was clearly settled by the *Plyler v. Doe* case (1982). The Supreme Court considered whether a state could withhold free public education from the undocumented children of alien parents. The Fourteenth Amendment states: "No state should . . . deprive any person of life, liberty or property without due process of law: nor deny to *any person within its jurisdiction* the equal protection of the laws." The Texas legislature reasoned that the undocumented aliens were not persons within their "jurisdiction." The Court stated simply, "We reject this argument." The principle that free public education is available to all children residing within the boundaries of the state was firmly established.

c. *Educating Children With AIDS*

The advent of AIDS among schoolchildren rekindled the question of whether a school district can exclude students for health reasons. The courts are uniform in their insistence that children with AIDS must be allowed to attend school in regular classrooms unless a child's condition requires an alternative placement. In the case of more readily contagious diseases, the school's responsibility is to provide adequate assignments at home for short illnesses or home instruction for longer illnesses (*Martinez v. School Board of Hillsboro County, Fla.,* 1988).

d. *Enforcing Immunizations*

States may require immunization for entering students. The courts support the state's compelling interest in controlling and preventing communicable diseases in the schools. The exception to this, of course, is the refusal to obtain the required immunizations based on religious beliefs. One interesting court decision further specified that the exemption be extended to all people who claim religious objections, not only to members of "recognized" religions (*Sherr v. Northport-East Northport Union Free School District,* 1987).

e. *Enforcing Minimum Education Standards*

States also have a compelling interest in their children receiving a standard minimum education whether this takes place in a public or private school. Based on this principle, recent court cases have upheld state regulations establishing instructional standards for private schools (*Fellowship Baptist Church v. Benton*, 1988). In other cases (*Duro v. District Attorney*, 1983), the courts have ruled that the exemption that the Supreme Court afforded the Amish, based on the exercise of the religion clause of the First Amendment, does not apply to most other religions. The key was the unique Amish way of life, including the rural setting.

F. The Limits on Home Schooling

More and more parents these days are opting for home schooling. Most states permit this under certain circumstances. Compulsory education is not a principle in common law. Rather, it is a feature of the state education code and/or constitution. Consequently, states are free to define a home school as a private school, regulated by state laws.

In California, home schooling by correspondence did not satisfy the court's interpretation of the compulsory education laws. The Supreme Court of Illinois, on the other hand, accepted instruction at home by a parent who had "two years of college and some training in pedagogy and educational psychology" (Reutter, 1985). The key is in the term *equivalent instruction*. School administrators have a professional and ethical obligation to assure that children within their jurisdiction are being properly educated. To fail in this responsibility is to allow some children to be denied their rights as U.S. citizens.

3.2 Spotting Traditional Legal Problems in the Curriculum

Education is a function of the state, and the state legislature has the power to determine what will be taught in its schools. School board members, as officers of the state, must provide instructional programs in the subjects required by the legislature. Wisely, legislatures have been reluctant to go further than prescribing subjects by title and defining the length of time to be devoted to instruction.

School boards, on the other hand, appropriately become more involved with courses of study and instructional objectives. Generally, when enacting laws concerning the curriculum, the legislatures have dealt with content rather than methodology. In other words, lawmakers deal primarily with *what* should be taught rather than *how* to teach it.

A. Curriculum Required by the State

The courts have supported both the general content role of the legislatures (Reutter, 1985) and the more specific roles of school boards and school personnel involving teaching methodology (*Robinson, Treasurer v. Schenck,* 1879). Furthermore, as noted previously in this chapter, pupils are required to take the subjects prescribed by the legislature. The courts have been very protective of the state's right to impose curricular requirements on the students attending its schools. The exception to this is when a personal constitutional right is involved. For example, a court intervened when a requirement to take ROTC violated the student's First Amendment rights to free exercise of religion (*Spence v. Bailey,* 1972). In another case, however, the court upheld a requirement to attend a class in which religious material was presented because there was no intent to indoctrinate and the relevant course material was taught in a constitutionally appropriate manner (*Vaughn v. Reed,* 1970).

B. Curriculum Required by the School Board

A question can be raised about the authority of local school boards to require attendance in certain specified courses, because the local board does not have the plenary power of the state. The question may be academic, however, because it is agreed that local school boards usually have the sole authority to grant a diploma. Hence it may not be possible to force a high school student to attend a local school board-required course, but the school board, in return, would not be required to issue a diploma to the student. In the absence of a statutory provision, parents may select the subjects for their children from the school's course of study.

c. *Graduation Requirements*

School districts have the authority to determine graduation requirements as long as they conform with the minimum state requirements. Once these have been adopted, they become more or less a contract with the pupil. If a pupil completes the requirements as specified by the local school board, the granting of a diploma is mandatory. This has caused frustration on the part of administrators charged with conducting decorous graduation ceremonies. Threatening to withhold diplomas for rowdyism may be an effective bluff, but it won't hold up in court.

D. *Classifying and Placing Students*

School boards have the general power to classify students. Their students may be retained, accelerated, or placed in special classes based on the educational judgment of professional personnel. Naturally, the courts will intervene if the school's staff abuses its authority, applies judgment arbitrarily, or violates a personal, constitutional right.

E. *Enforcing School Attendance Areas*

Likewise, school boards have the authority to assign students to specific school facilities. School attendance areas may be established by the board and then changed at a later date. Generally, parents have no recourse in court, even when the real estate agent guarantees the home to be in the attendance area of a prestige school. Again, the exception is when the attendance boundaries infringe upon personal constitutional rights (for example, by creating segregated schools).

F. *Promoting and Retaining Students*

Placement of students in schools or classes based on test scores has been increasingly challenged in recent years. The cultural biases of tests often left schools with segregated classes, resulting in court censure. The courts have been consistent in upholding placement based on achievement or ability, however, as long as the methods for determining these qualities are not biased. This practice of segregation, like the practice of retention, may disappear as a result of condemnation by education professionals. A mounting body of evidence indicates that the practice of retention is ineffective at best and counterproductive at worst. Knowledgeable educators believe that the practice will soon be abandoned entirely. Likewise, the damage caused by segregation is no less real when it is caused by low ability or low achievement. In a case involving a special honors preparatory school in a public school system, the use of grade point averages as criteria for admission to a public school was upheld by the courts even though the practice created de facto segregation (*Berkelman v. San Francisco Unified School District,* 1974). Students of school law now speculate that the limited impact on the remaining students in the district probably had an influence on this case.

G. *Coping With Sex Education*

Any time schools deal with sex or religion, the potential for inspiring emotional responses from community groups is high. The question of whether sex education should be part of a public school curriculum has been firmly decided. Generally, neither the rights of the parents nor the rights of the students are violated by the teaching of "family life" or sex education, as long as the parents have the right to have their children excused from instruction. This does not mean that the parents have the right to waive a semester-long health course. Rather, parents have the right to have their children excused from that portion of the class dealing with sex and family life. Many states have spelled out in statute the procedures for alerting parents to family life course content, explaining the curriculum and materials, and providing alternate instruction. The key to avoiding problems in this area, most wizened school administrators agree, is good communication with parents and a willingness to accommodate the family's concerns.

H. *Spotting Bias in the Curriculum*

Good educational practice and law demand that educators examine their materials and curricula to eliminate damaging stereotypes. In most cases, school administrators can accomplish this by raising the awareness of the professional staff. An imbalance of material or a slant to instruction that fails to portray races and genders in the full spectrum of vocational and professional roles is potentially damaging to the vulnerable personalities in our classrooms.

I. *Dealing With Family Values, Self-Esteem, and Secular Humanism*

Locally managed public school systems will always be the target of attacks by well-meaning citizens who believe that students should be subject to a certain amount of indoctrination for their own good. Consequently, free and open discussion of certain sensitive areas, particularly politics, religion, and sex, will often generate strong responses that must be managed skillfully by school personnel. The last three decades have witnessed attacks on various aspects of the curriculum. For example, global education was attacked for failing to emphasize American nationalism, and self-esteem activities, for failure to include the absolute nature of right and wrong. Secular humanism has been attacked for failure to endorse religion or for being a "substitute" religion. Virtually every area of the instructional program, including math, science, social science, and English, has been criticized for conflicting with religion. Fortunately, the courts offer the beleaguered schools some protection. The Supreme Court has established, as a guideline, the principle that courts should not intervene in the daily operation of the schools unless a basic constitutional right is involved. In 1967, however, the Court declared that it will not "tolerate laws which cast a pall of orthodoxy over the classroom." Nor will it permit rules or state laws that tend to restrict knowledge (*Meyer v. State of Nebraska*, 1923).

Consequently, attempts to limit the freedom of teachers to responsibly conduct their profession have been stymied by the courts. Nevertheless, the best solution to the problem of this sort between schools and communities is a rational, sympathetic, and widespread program of parent and community communications to ward off the expensive, time-consuming, and nonproductive court confrontation.

3.3 Managing Grades, Tests, and Student Records

A. *Grading*

The courts usually will not interfere in the school's policies and procedures for grading student performance. On rare occasions, the courts have intervened when the school was arbitrary or capricious in assigning grades. For example, reduction of a student's grade for violating school rules that were not related to the classroom instruction was deemed to be an illegal application of the school district's discretion (*Katzman v. Cumberland Valley School District*, 1984). Some states have laws regulating grading practices, and the courts will intervene if a school district violates them. For example, California's Education Code forbids the bureaucracy from changing the grade assigned from a teacher except in the case of clerical mistake, fraud, bad faith, or incompetency. The courts also may intervene if a school assigns grades to students in a manner that violates the district's policies.

Student grades will always be a sensitive area prone to conflict between students, families, and schools. The best defense is a clear set of grading policies and procedures that are communicated to the staff, students, and parents in advance.

B. *Testing*

The courts also are reluctant to become involved with student testing, unless the use of the test data results in racial, ethnic, or gender segregation. The landmark *Larry P.* case (1984) in

California ruled that the use of standardized IQ tests for the placement of students in classes for the mentally retarded was unconstitutional. The court based its decision on the fact that black children made up 25% of the students identified as mentally retarded, while only 10% of the school-age population of the state was black. In other words, *the tests were biased and resulted in unconstitutional segregation.* Recently, however, the Larry P. judge has decided to allow school districts to administer IQ tests to black children upon parent request.

Teacher-made tests to evaluate student progress are virtually immune to successful court challenges unless they are in violation of state law or district policy or they are used to unconstitutionally segregate the students.

c. Keeping Student Records Confidential

State legislatures have uniformly adopted rules and regulations conforming with the Family Educational Rights and Privacy Act of 1974, also known as the Buckley Amendment. Like other federal laws related to education, the Buckley Amendment applies only to schools receiving federal funding. As previously noted, however, this is a moot point, because virtually all public schools and many private schools receive federal funding in one form or another, and most state legislatures have adopted parallel legislation. In general, the amendment requires the following:

Student records must be kept confidential. The exception to this is so-called directory information, which may be released to prospective employers, colleges and universities, and representatives of the news media. Also included in this exception are the data normally associated with athletic rosters and academic honor rolls. Administrators should be careful that these directory lists do not identify students to a greater degree than the law permits or that the information released is contrary to the best interests of the students. For example, posting the grade averages of the football team or listing the final exam grades for a class could be potentially harmful to the student and thus in violation of the Buckley Amendment. Parents and adult students (age 18) must be given an annual opportunity to prohibit release of directory information.

Parents must be allowed to inspect and challenge the information kept in their child's records. Naturally, care must be taken to be certain that the persons inspecting the student records are actually the parents or the legal guardians.

Key Terms

- ☐ *Biased curriculum.* Slanted instruction or instructional material that fails to portray nationalities, races, or genders in a full spectrum of social, vocational, and professional roles.
- ☐ *Buckley Amendment.* The Family Educational Right to Privacy Act of 1974, which establishes standards for access to student and family information collected by the school district.
- ☐ *Compulsory education.* State statutes that require children of specified ages to attend school.
- ☐ *Emancipated minor.* Status granted to minors that declares them free from the control of their parents.
- ☐ *Equivalent instruction.* The test applied by courts to determine whether home schooling satisfies the state's compulsory education laws with regard to the qualifications of staff and the instructional program.
- ☐ *Family life courses.* A euphemism for *sex education.*
- ☐ *Global education.* An interdisciplinary approach to social science that emphasizes the interdependence of all peoples.
- ☐ *Promotion.* The assignment of students to the next grade level.
- ☐ *Retention.* The assignment of students to the same grade level for a second year.
- ☐ *School attendance areas.* Geographic areas designated by local school boards for the purpose of dividing the school population among several school facilities.
- ☐ *Secular humanism.* Generally a term applied to some of the social sciences, particularly studies dealing with the personality; sometimes attacked as an "atheistic religion."
- ☐ *Student classification and placement.* The acts of local school districts to assign students to appropriate-level classes and programs.

References

Berkelman v. San Francisco Unified School District, 501 F.2d 1264 (9th Cir. 1974).

Davis v. Meek, 344 F. Supp. 198 (N.D. Ohio 1972).

Duro v. District Attorney, Second Judicial Dist. of North Carolina, 721 F.2d 96 (4th Cir. 1983).

Fellowship Baptist Church v. Benton, 678 F. Supp. 213 (S.D. Iowa 1988)

Katzman v. Cumberland Valley School District, 479 A.2d 671 (Pa. Cmwlth. 1984).

Larry P. v. Riles, 793 F.2d 969 (9th Cir. 1984).

Martinez v. School Board of Hillsboro County, Fla., 861 F.2d 1502 (11th Cir. 1988).

Meyer v. State of Nebraska, 262 U.S. 390, 43 S.Ct. 625 (1923).

Plyler v. Doe, 457 U.S. 202, 102 S.Ct. 2382 72 L.Ed. 2d 786 (1982).

Reutter, E. E. (1985). *The law of public education* (3rd ed.). Mineola, NY: Foundation Press.

Robinson, Treasurer v. Schenck, 102 Indiana 307 (1879).

Sherr v. Northport-East Northport Union Free School District., 672 F. Supp. 81 (E.D. N.Y. 1987).

Spence v. Bailey, 465 F.2d 797 (6th Cir. 1972).

Vaughn v. Reed, 313 F. Supp. 431 (W.D. Va. 1970).

4

Planning for Good School Discipline

4.1 Planning a Team Approach

Few characteristics of a school are more basic to the conduct of education than good school discipline. As one experienced professional noted, "It isn't the most important thing we do; but until order is established, nothing else will be accomplished." Because administrators are ultimately responsible for the conduct of effective school operations, planning for good school discipline begins with them. Ultimately, however, it involves every member of the staff: the teachers, the custodians, the secretaries, the aides, and the administrators.

4.2 Developing Strong Board Policies

Planning for good school discipline begins with good school board policy empowering administrators and teachers to deal with the multiplicity of behavior problems faced in modern American schools. These policies typically delegate to the staff the responsibility for maintaining good student discipline. They usually contain guidelines and processes for disciplinary action such as the grounds for suspension, expulsion, the limits on detention and other punishments, the district's requirements for notifying parents, and board requirements for addressing student behavior problems of special local importance.

4.3 Designing Comprehensive Site Discipline Plans

Ultimately, student discipline is the responsibility of the site staff. An effective school discipline plan is the result of a school administrator's working diligently with all constituents of the school community: the teachers, parents, students, district administrators, business people, residents, police, and social workers.

A. *Develop a Code of Student Behavior*

The first step is to identify the possible problem areas and draft a code of student behavior for discussion by faculty, students, police, community advisory groups, and the school district's attorney. Reducing school rules and regulations to concise written statements is an important part of the Supreme Court's substantive due process requirements described in detail later in this chapter.

B. *Involve the Staff and Community*

The next step is to gather advice and input from as many sectors of the community as possible for use by the staff in adopting the final code of student behavior. The result should be a written set of rules, regulations, consequences, and processes that are fully supported by the staff responsible for enforcing them. The resulting code should be reviewed and discussed regularly with members of the staff. The entire process should be repeated every three or four years to maintain the strong support of the full community.

c. *Publish the Code*

The next step is to publish and circulate the written rules and regulations. Then, establish a process for orienting the teachers, parents, and larger community. This has been done successfully in a number of ways. The most formal method is to publish a student handbook that contains not only the school rules but also other useful information about the school such as activities, schedules, calendars, and so forth. Typically, these handbooks are distributed to students at the beginning of the year and discussed in class by the teachers. Some staffs go a step further by testing the students to assure a high level of understanding of the behavior code and other school processes.

D. *Communicate With the Public*

Finally, the school disciplinary code should be communicated to the parents and the wider community. Including school discipline as a part of parent orientation programs and bulletins is a good beginning. One successful principal in a suburban high school found that mailing a summary version of the school code to all residents in his attendance area reaped big dividends in school support. The residents were accustomed to stories of disruptive behavior in the nation's schools and assumed that the local high school was part of it. They were gratified to learn that the local school demanded orderly behavior from the students.

The written code of behavior also should be distributed to all members of the staff, both certified and noncertified. A faculty handbook is probably the most convenient location for information of this sort. Included with the rules and regulations should be guidelines for faculty response to various problematic student behaviors. Again, the key is good orientation. Periodic whole-faculty discussions and other means of communication about the purposes and processes of the disciplinary plan are essential.

The importance of full staff cooperation in establishing good school discipline can't be overemphasized. An alert staff can prevent major problems developing from minor disciplinary infractions. As one successful school principal put it, "Many students learn good school behavioral habits simply because they don't have opportunities to misbehave."

4.4 Protecting Student Rights

School administrators have the duty to provide a safe, orderly campus for the conduct of schooling. They also are responsible for protecting the students who attend the schools. In years past, the relationship of school personnel to pupils was likened to the relationship of parents to children. In recent years, however, the conventional notion of educators standing in place of parents, or *in loco parentis,* has changed. School administrators have been forced to be more sensitive to individual rights guaranteed by the Constitution to their students. As the following paragraphs will demonstrate, this does not mean that administrators are stripped of their authority to control and regulate students. Rather, it means that the approach must take into consideration the rights of the individual as well as the welfare of the institution.

4.5 Guaranteeing Due Process

The U.S. Constitution guarantees that the law will treat all people fairly and equally. The Fourteenth Amendment prescribes "due process of law" before any person may be deprived of "life, liberty or property." Until the early 1960s, the courts were reluctant to question the authority of schools. Education was considered a privilege, not a right. Locally controlled school districts were deemed to have the authority to deny attendance if educating the student would be unusually expensive or if the student had violated certain school rules. Beginning with the *Dixon v. Alabama State* case (1961), the court began constructing a framework that would eventually affect all schools in the nation. The language of the court of appeals described attendance at a public institution as a "right." "It requires no argument to demonstrate that education is vital. . . . Without sufficient education the plaintiffs would not be able to earn an adequate livelihood." The court continued by outlining the minimum "due process" procedures before a student could be deprived of education. These included the following:

- an opportunity to hear the charges and learn the names of the witnesses and
- an opportunity to present a defense to an administrative official.

In 1975, the Supreme Court ruled in *Goss v. Lopez* that minimum procedural due process must be afforded students in the public schools before they can be suspended even for a short period of time.

A. *Procedural Due Process*

The courts tend to require more due process procedures when the deprivation is greater, and less when the deprivation is smaller. For example, expelling the student from school for a year would require written notices, sufficient time for preparing a defense, a hearing, and the possible use of an attorney. A one-day suspension, on the other hand, would usually only require that students be given the opportunity to hear the charges from an administrator and to tell their side of the story.

B. *Substantive Due Process*

The courts have expanded procedural due process into a doctrine known as *substantive due process*. This can be summarized as "fair play." Essentially, this doctrine prescribes the following:

- The people involved in any procedural due process should be impartial.
- The laws, rules, and regulations that are the subject of the disciplinary hearing should be written and clear.
- The evidence and witnesses against the accused should be revealed to the accused.

4.6 Protecting Freedom of Speech

Of all the freedoms Americans enjoy, none is cherished so much as freedom of speech. Oliver Wendell Holmes, Sr., put it best when he said, "The very aim and end of our institutions is this: that we may think what we like and say what we think." It should not have been a surprise to school administrators when the Supreme Court reminded them "that neither students nor teachers shed their constitutional rights to freedom of speech or expression at the schoolhouse gate" (*Tinker v. Des Moines I.C.S.D.*, 1969). In addition to the guarantees of the federal Constitution, student free speech rights often are expressly guaranteed by state statutes enacted in response to the High Court's direction.

Freedom of speech in American schools, like freedom of speech in American society, is not absolute. Moreover, the school setting is fraught with seemingly competing values and demands. For example, our society encourages schools to develop freethinking, risk-taking, freedom-loving adults while at the same time demanding that schools be orderly and disciplined and that proper morals and manners be instilled. The following paragraphs describe the position of the Court concerning speech-related activities regularly encountered on school campuses.

A. Saluting the Flag

The Supreme Court and lower courts have consistently ruled that neither students nor teachers may be compelled to salute the flag (*West Virginia State Board of Education v. Barnette*, 1943). For similar reasons, the courts have found it unconstitutional to force students to stand while the pledge is being recited (*Banks v. Board of Public Instruction*, 1970). Although the courts will not require a teacher to stand or lead a class in the Pledge of Allegiance, it is reasonable to expect the teacher to make arrangements for the pledge to be taught and led, either by one of the students or by another teacher on the staff.

B. Buttons, Badges, and Other Insignia

In the landmark *Tinker v. Des Moines I.C.S.D.* case (1969), the U.S. Supreme Court justices declared that the high school students who wore black arm-bands to protest the Vietnam war were exercising their right to free speech. Consequently, the school should not have abridged that right unless there was a "clear and present danger" that the speech would substantially disrupt school and interfere with the conduct of education.

C. Dress Codes

The "school disruption" standard has been used to judge the constitutionality of school dress and grooming codes. Court decisions in this area have made it clear, however, that student rights are far from absolute. If the apparel or grooming practice disrupts the classroom or infringes on the rights of other students, it is clearly not protected.

D. Gang Colors and Insignia

The court reinforced the school's authority to regulate dress in the *Guzick* case by upholding a school rule that banned buttons and insignias (*Guzick v. Drebus*, 1970). The court recognized that, because of the racial tension involved on the campus, the rules were necessary. Insignias would exacerbate racial problems and presented a "clear and present danger" to the safe conduct of schooling. For this reason, school officials can feel comfortable in banning gang "colors," jackets, and other identifying articles of clothing or insignias when the presence of gangs or secret fraternities threatens to disrupt the school or abridge the rights of other students.

E. Sexual References and Use of Profanity

The courts have been very consistent in supporting the regulation of student speech to maintain order. School administrators have the authority to forbid profanity and abusive language (*Burnside v. Byers*, 1956). Speech containing sexual innuendo is more difficult to control. A Supreme Court decision, however, upheld the disciplinary measures applied to a student who made a speech replete with sexual innuendos in a school assembly. The Court ruled that even a mild disruption in this instance was sufficient to justify the student's suspension (*Bethel School District v. Fraser,* 1986). Application of this holding depends on the extent to which state law protects student speech.

F. Demonstrations

The U.S. Supreme Court has ruled that peaceful student demonstrations are protected by the Constitution. This protection is also extended to nonstudents who choose to demonstrate or picket on the sidewalks next to the school (*Grayned v. City of Rockford,* 1972). This does not mean, however, that instruction can be disrupted at will. Quite the contrary, the Court emphasized that exercise of free speech in this manner is not protected because the school could not be expected to "tolerate boisterous demonstrators who drown out classroom conversation, make studying impossible, block entrances, or incite children to leave the schoolhouse" (*Grayned,* 1972). School administrators, however, should guard against overreaction to student demonstrations. Law enforcement officials remind us that peaceful demonstrations often act as a safety valve and possibly prevent full-blown riots.

G. *Student Publications*

In general, the columnists for student newspapers enjoy protected free speech rights. Administrators may intervene and exert control, or "prior restraint," only when the publication threatens to disrupt the instructional program. As noted previously, administrators also are empowered to bar students from using lewd or indecent speech, whether written or spoken. Moreover, a staff adviser to student publications has the duty to teach responsible journalism and to supervise the products of the student staff.

H. *Student Expression*

Student expression that is obscene, libelous, or slanderous also can be prohibited; however, determining what is obscene, libelous, or slanderous can be tricky. The best advice to an administrator is to check with the school district's attorney. School administrators find editorial attacks against staff members to be particularly disturbing, especially if the scurrilous editorials are aimed at the administrators themselves. Unless the publication is profane, or criticizes in a vulgar manner, however, chances are it is protected by the First Amendment. Responsible journalism should allow a reply by those attacked in such a manner.

I. *Student Distribution of Literature*

Students have a fundamental First Amendment right to distribute handbills, leaflets, and pamphlets containing information and opinions on virtually any subject (*Mandel v. Municipal Court,* 1970). The task that faces school administrators is one of regulation and control. The free speech right does not, for example, permit students to cause a litter problem for the grounds crew.

J. *Banning Books or Removing Books From the Library*

As a rule, local school boards have a great deal of discretion concerning the school district's curriculum and the textbooks to be used in the classroom. Subject only to the demands and restrictions of the state legislature, the school board has more or less absolute authority to reject or adopt classroom texts. This authority to remove books from the library, however, is somewhat limited. In the *Board of Education v. Pico* case (1982), the U.S. Supreme Court ruled that freedom to receive information and ideas is a corollary of freedom of speech and press. Hence it is protected by the First Amendment. This does not mean that boards are required to purchase library books willy-nilly based on the requests of students. Rather, the decision was aimed at preventing boards from removing books from the school library in order to deny the students access to information and ideas with which the board members disagree.

Prior to this decision, it was a common practice for school administrators or school boards to remove books from the library after being informed of "inappropriate" content. The *Pico* decision declared that a "regime of voluntary inquiry" exists in the library. Therefore removing books to deny students access to ideas is a violation of their First Amendment rights. It is important to note that the Court action focused on *removing* books from the library. The decision does not restrict the board and administrator's authority to establish criteria for selecting library books, nor does it restrict the administrator's obligation to supervise the selection process to ensure a well-balanced library collection and the best use of limited school dollars.

Banning videotapes and other classroom materials. The technological explosion during the past two decades has created new opportunities for teachers to make greater use of various media in the classroom. The proliferation of commercial videotape libraries has caused headaches as well as opportunities for administrators. A Southern California school district was sued by the parents of a child who allegedly suffered emotional

trauma as a result of viewing an inappropriate videotape in one
of her high school classes. The plaintiffs argued that the board
and administrators had not lived up to their responsibility to
regulate these materials. In this case, the matter was settled out
of court, and no limits on the school district's responsibility to
control such materials were defined. Wizened school administrators, however, feel that establishing a structure that relies
upon individual teacher judgment in consultation with school
administrators is probably the most workable approach. It is
neither possible nor desirable to establish rules requiring
administrative approval of all classroom materials used by cre-
ative teachers. In the final analysis, the teacher's good judgment is the critical factor. The board and administrators can
properly support and enhance this teacher judgment by providing clear written guidelines and by involving staff members in
periodic staff development activities to heighten awareness of
potential problems and pitfalls.

4.7 Using Proper Search and Seizure Procedures

The courts have wisely recognized that school authorities
need considerable constitutional leeway to protect their students and provide a safe, orderly environment for education.
For example, prudent administrators frequently find it necessary to search students or student lockers. Although the U.S.
Supreme Court ruled that the Fourth Amendment prohibition
of unreasonable searches and seizures *does* apply to public
school officials, it added that the search warrant process was
unworkable in the school setting. Therefore the only test school
authorities must meet is whether or not the search is "reasonable" under the circumstances (*New Jersey v. T.L.O.*, 1985). Administrators should also keep in mind that the conduct of a
search should not be "excessively intrusive in light of the age
and sex of the student and the nature of the infraction." A strip
search of a 13-year-old girl suspected of possessing drugs was
clearly beyond the authority of the school administrators.

4.8 Mass Searches and Locker Searches

The courts have sanctioned mass searches of lockers and automobiles. Searches of groups of students, however, can only be conducted when school personnel have "reasonable" cause. For example, if an administrator heard a rumor that one of the students on a school bus was carrying an explosive device, it would be "reasonable" cause to search the students on the bus. On the other hand, randomly searching students to "prevent" them from bringing drugs on campus is not reasonable. Using dogs to "sniff out" drugs in lockers or cars is permitted; using them to "sniff out" drugs on students is not.

4.9 Enforcing School Rules

Processes for enforcing school rules and regulations must be established with the students' rights in mind. To be most effective, these processes should regularly be the subject of staff in-service training sessions attended by the administrators and teachers as well as by the noncertified staff. Good school discipline is a whole-staff effort. Failure on the part of a staff member to observe proper disciplinary processes not only results in unfairness to the student but also threatens to undermine the entire staff by embroiling the school in nonproductive conflicts with parents.

4.10 Crimes on Campus

Schools are not sanctuaries for criminal behavior. Crimes committed by students often must be reported to the police for full prosecution. In a number of cases, the student activities are clearly crimes, such as selling drugs, using dangerous weapons, or setting off explosives. In other cases, the educator is faced with deciding whether the activity is a schoolyard scuffle or assault and battery. Our advice is to err on the side of dealing

too strictly with potentially criminal behavior. Anyone who has
ever been tormented by the classroom bully will agree that all
educators have a basic duty to protect their students from in-
fringement of their rights as human beings. Few of us would
agree to work for an organization that allowed its employees to
threaten or assault one another. We would insist that management take action to ensure decent working conditions. School
administrators can do no less.

Criminal law is usually not applicable to students under 16
years of age; however, the laws governing education in all states
contain rules and regulations that charge school officials with
the task of preventing antisocial and criminal behavior by their
students. These laws also specify these behaviors as grounds for
disciplinary action including permanent expulsion from a public school system.

A. *Fights and Assaults*

Conflicts between students that result in violence are the
most serious breaches of student discipline faced by school administrators. It is puzzling that educators frequently show tol-
erance for such behavior. "Trivial playground scuffles" can
rapidly escalate into major confrontations resulting in injuries
and death. Worse yet, the school environment loses an important quality of being a safe place to learn. All states allow the
full range of disciplinary action for campus violence. Our advice
is to crack down on fighting and assaults at the very beginning.
Educators at any level cannot tolerate assaultive behavior by
students.

Law enforcement makes a distinction between "assault" and
"battery." An assault is an *attempt* to commit a battery. In other
words, if the school bully chases his victim until the playground
supervisor intervenes, he has committed an assault. Similarly,
students who challenge other students to fight or badger them
until they are provoked to fight also are guilty of criminal behavior in most states under laws dealing with disturbing the
peace or, in the case of California, an old law designed to sup-

press gunfighting. These low levels of misbehavior should be seriously considered in a comprehensive school disciplinary plan.

B. *Weapons*

The presence of weapons on the school campus creates a threat to the safety and welfare of all students. In this respect, it is similar to threatening or assaultive student behavior. Consequently, even seemingly minor infractions must be taken seriously to prevent an "arms race." Education codes in all states allow the full range of disciplinary action to be taken against students possessing weapons on campus. In California, administrators are required by law to report weapons infractions to the school board for the possible expulsion of students from the district. Weapons include any instrument carried by a student *to be used as a weapon.* For example, a student who brings a tire iron on campus could be subject to the same penalties as the student who brings a gun, knife, or billy club. The keys to weapon control on campus are vigilance by all staff and swift, certain action by administrators.

C. *Explosives and Firecrackers*

Persons who bring explosives onto the school campus may be guilty of a felony. The detonation of firecrackers on campus or at school events is an extremely serious offense. School laws permit the full range of disciplinary action to be taken against students found possessing or detonating explosives of any type on school campuses.

D. *Child Abuse*

All states have laws that require school employees to report child abuse. Whenever a teacher, administrator, or school nurse has a *reasonable suspicion* that a person under 18 years of age has been abused, a report must be filed with the local law enforcement agency or the county welfare department within a reasonable period of time (usually 24 to 48 hours). Failure to report suspected child abuse can result in criminal penalties that include hefty fines and/or jail time. In addition, the person who fails to file a report may incur a personal civil liability when the family of the victim sues for damages (*Landeros v. Flood,* 1975).

Recognizing the signs of child abuse. Child abuse most often involves cruelty to a child by an adult in the household. School employees have a reason to suspect child abuse when a child reports to school with bruises or lacerations—especially if this is a frequent occurrence. Child abuse also includes intentional injury by someone on the playground, willful neglect by the parents, sexual assault, and mental cruelty. Neglect and nonaccidental injuries are relatively easy to spot. Sexual assault or mental abuse is more difficult and may require special training to properly equip the staff with the skills to identify the symptoms.

Providing adequate staff training. In California recently, failure to provide proper instructions to the school staff regarding child abuse laws (including in-service training) caused the responsible administrators to suffer penalties including suspension of their credentials. The key is in the phrase *reasonable suspicion.* For example, if a victimized child's playmate discloses to a teacher that sexual or mental abuse has taken place, the teacher definitely has a reason to suspect and is obliged by law to report the suspicion to the local law enforcement agency or the county welfare department.

Often, the adults reported to the law enforcement agencies for suspected child abuse are enraged and threaten the school district and staff with lawsuits. Child abuse laws, however, protect the people making the reports by granting them immunity to lawsuits, unless, of course, the report is made maliciously for the purpose of harassing the accused. In most states, the names of child abuse reporters remain confidential and are not released to the person being investigated.

E. *Hazing*

Hazing is characterized as an activity that is likely to "cause bodily danger or personal degradation or disgrace resulting in physical or mental harm to any fellow student" (*California Education Code 32051*). Laws throughout the United States prohibit hazing in public schools. School officials who condone activities of this sort are subject to criminal penalties and civil lawsuits for personal liability. The in-service training for staff concerning good school discipline should emphasize the recognition as well as the prevention of hazing. Faculty who would immediately stop an upper-class person from paddling a first-year student may not recognize that pulling this person's pants down or forcing him or her to do humiliating tasks may be just as dangerous and damaging. Similar to in-service training for staff concerning child abuse, it is the responsibility of administrators to educate their staffs about the prevention of hazing.

F. *Theft, Robbery, Extortion*

A theft occurs when one student takes another student's property. Theft also occurs if a student finds another student's lost property and makes no attempt to find the owner.

More serious in the school setting is robbery or extortion. A robbery occurs when property is taken from a person by force or threat. Blackmailing students or forcing students to pay "protection" are examples of extortion. All of these infractions, including receiving stolen property, are causes for disciplinary action under the laws governing education. If the students are over 16 years of age, they may also be liable for criminal prosecution.

G. *Vandalism*

Schools are frequently targets for vandalism. School officials are custodians of the public's property and must take whatever steps necessary to prevent vandalism and to preserve property. Most states have stringent laws against vandalism of public facilities. Site administrators have successfully employed several strategies to suppress vandalism. These include the following:

- Investigate vigorously each instance of vandalism to identify the miscreants, then prosecute to the limit of the law.
- If the vandals are students, insist that the parents make reparations (many state laws render parents liable if their children damage public property).
- Offer a reward. In California, the parents or guardian of the vandals are also liable for the amount of the reward up to $5,000.
- Enlist the support of the students through campus beautification projects and classroom discussions.
- Bring a couple of members of the grounds crew on campus early before school starts to inspect the facilities and remove all evidence of vandalism before the students arrive. "Vandalism breeds more vandalism" is an axiom among administrators of vandalism-prone schools. Quick repairs lessen the impact, and consequently the incidents do not serve as inspiration to other would-be vandals.

H. Drugs, Alcohol, and Tobacco

Politicians and educational leaders have declared substance abuse to be the greatest problem facing America's youth today. Public school officials have been saddled with two missions. The first is to provide a school environment free of dangerous substances. The second is to equip students with the understandings and principles necessary to avoid abusing these substances. Both tasks are monumental in their proportions.

Keeping a drug-free campus. With regard to keeping the campus drug- and alcohol-free, the law offers firm support. Major penalties are associated with the sale, possession, or use of drugs, alcohol, and tobacco on campus. School boards and administrators have taken extraordinary measures to keep their campuses clean. These include breathalizers to check for alco-

hol use, trained dogs to "sniff out" drugs in lockers and automobiles, closed campuses with secure fences to prevent dealers
from entering (and students from leaving to meet the dealers),
"stings" by undercover officers posing as students, and generally heightened surveillance by staff.

All states authorize a full range of disciplinary action for drug
involvement. California law mandates that students found selling drugs be referred to the school board for possible expulsion.

Teaching substance abuse prevention. Drug and alcohol
abuse prevention programs generally have not achieved mea-
surable success in reducing the incidence of drug abuse. At the
current time, school efforts aimed at reshaping problematic student personality characteristics associated with drug abuse
seem promising. Experiments with cooperative learning groups
and other school activities requiring positive social interaction
have demonstrated significant progress in reducing factors that
lead to substance abuse such as school alienation and social iso-
lation (Solomon, Watson, Delucchi, Schaps, & Battistich, 1988).

I. Disobedience, Defiance, and Disruption

The laws of the states delegate to the local school officials the
authority to establish rules and regulations necessary to conduct school, including the rules and regulations for student conduct that constitute a school's discipline plan. With minor
exceptions, the states allow the full range of penalties against
students who defy the valid authority of school personnel or who
disobey the valid rules of conduct designed by the staff. As we
have noted previously, school rules and regulations are not valid
if they violate a student's constitutional rights. For example,
students cannot be disciplined for disobeying a rule requiring
them to stand for the Pledge of Allegiance. They also cannot be
denied admission to school for refusing to obey the immunization laws, if the refusal is based on religious convictions protected by the Constitution.

J. Off-Campus Offenses

Students may be disciplined for unacceptable conduct off campus or on weekends and vacations *if it is related to school attendance.* The courts have consistently upheld the right of school officials to punish students who harass their classmates on the way home from school or who arrange to finish a playground fight on the weekend to avoid the school's authority (*O'Rourke v. Walker,* 1925).

K. Truancy

Chapter 3 discussed the state's power to enforce school attendance laws. Full-time school attendance is compulsory in most states for students between the ages of 6 and 16. Students who disobey these laws are truants and subject to the full range of school discipline as well as possible penalties imposed by law enforcement agencies. Normally, school administrators are reluctant to suspend students for truancy because a suspension results in additional school time missed. In California, the state's laws prohibit suspension or expulsion as penalties for truancy or tardiness to class. Consequently, many schools use "in-house suspensions" or detention as alternatives to suspension for truancy or tardiness.

4.11 Administering Punishment Effectively

School rules and regulations are frequently enforced by administering punishment to the students breaking the rules. The forms of punishment commonly include removal of privileges, detention, short-term suspension, long-term expulsion, and, in some cases, corporal punishment.

A. Removal of Privileges

The range of sanctions imposed by school personnel to discipline students is broad. Usually the courts impose no special conditions on the use of minor sanctions. A teacher is free to take away a student's free reading privilege or remove the student from a playground game without due process. As the penalties become more severe, however, an informal hearing may be required. For example, a principal could be required to explain charges being brought against students and allow them to explain their behavior before denying them the privilege of participating in a class field trip. Barring a student from participating on an athletic team or from participating in graduation ceremonies represents even more serious punishment and, consequently, requires that the school authorities be on procedurally solid ground. The disciplinary action should be justified by an infraction of a written regulation, and it must not be arbitrary, capricious, or unreasonable. In these cases, parents should be given an opportunity to discuss the matter with the administrator prior to the disciplinary action. There are a variety of school privileges and activities that, if taken away from students, have serious impact. These include drama and music activities, ceremonies of various sorts, school bus privileges, lunch hours and recesses, and participation in student government or other extracurricular activities.

B. Suspension

Suspension is distinguished from expulsion by the length of time a student is forbidden to attend school. Suspensions usually are for periods of 1 or 2 days but no more than 10 days. Expulsions usually are for a semester or more.

Limits on suspension. Some states limit the number of days a student can be suspended. New Jersey, for example, requires school board action before a student may be suspended more than 21 days. California limits suspensions to 5 days and further requires that the total suspensions in one year may not exceed 20 days.

Due process for suspensions. The U.S. Supreme Court has ruled that a student's entitlement to a public education is a "property interest" that is protected by the due process clause. Consequently, it may not be taken away for misconduct without at least the minimum procedures required by this constitutional provision (*Goss v. Lopez*, 1975). For suspensions of more than 10 days, courts have held that students have a right to a formal hearing and may be represented by a lawyer. Moreover, school authorities must keep an electronic or written record of these hearings to facilitate the appeal process.

These formal procedures are not required for suspensions of fewer than 10 days. Administrators must, however, provide for informal hearings that include adequate notices of the charges against the students and an opportunity to counter the charges. The U.S. Supreme Court allows the notices to be given to students orally. Most states and local districts, however, have adopted additional statutes or regulations requiring administrators to follow specific procedures that include written notice to parents.

Suspension is a serious consequence for misbehavior. Like expulsion, it should be used only when other means of correction fail. In several states, the law forbids suspension for minor school rule violations on the first offense unless other corrective measures have been attempted unsuccessfully. We advise that administrators review carefully and often the guidelines established by the state and school board for disciplinary action involving suspension. The principles of due process require that administrators faithfully comply with all of the state and local laws and regulations.

c. Expulsion

Expulsion differs from suspension in the length of time involved. Usually students are expelled for at least a semester, sometimes for an entire school year. Often a hearing for readmission is required. Because expulsion is a more severe disciplinary action than suspension, a greater degree of procedural due process is necessary. Unlike suspensions, which are the acts of administrators and staff, expulsions are normally carried out by the school board. The entire process is governed by prescribed guidelines in state law and board policy. We advise careful review of these procedural guidelines *before* an expulsion is imminent.

D. *Corporal Punishment*

In states where corporal punishment is permitted by law, the courts have supported its use. When applied reasonably, it is not "cruel or unusual," nor is it a violation of the student's due process rights. It is not surprising that the courts have frowned on excessively cruel punishment or physical acts that have caused serious injury to the students. For example, an Illinois court rejected the practice of using an electrical cattle prod on students, and a Texas court ruled against a football coach whose disciplinary measures sent one of his young charges to the hospital for several days.

Use established processes. Corporal punishment is normally governed by regulations in state law and school board policy. If staff members choose to use this disciplinary measure, we advise that the duly established processes be carefully observed. Preferably, the punishment should be administered by one of the school administrators in the presence of a disinterested witness.

Running laps. Corporal punishment is not limited to paddlings. It also includes running wind sprints, doing push-ups, running laps, and so forth—any *physical* punishment. The same rules apply to these forms of corporal punishment. In states where corporal punishment is prohibited, it is especially important that staff members be aware that the use of physical activities such as running laps as punishment is forbidden.

E. *Detention*

Most states allow school staff to keep students after school to finish their assignments or as punishment. Like the other traditional forms of school discipline, most states have rules and regulations governing the practice. State school board regulations in California, for instance, specify that a student may not be detained for more than one hour after school for disciplinary reasons.

Key Terms

- ❏ *Assault.* An attempt to commit a battery.
- ❏ *Battery.* Unlawful use of force or violence against another person.
- ❏ *Board policies.* Term applied to the codified rules, regulations, and directives of a local school board.
- ❏ *Child abuse.* Any mental or physical abuse or neglect of a minor by another person.
- ❏ *Code of behavior.* A codified set of rules and regulations governing behavior of students, usually developed at the school site level, often based on school board policy.
- ❏ *Corporal punishment.* Punishment inflicted on the body—a spanking, for example.
- ❏ *Criminal law.* Penal code law generally not applicable to students under 16 years of age.
- ❏ *Detention.* A punishment requiring a student to remain at school after school hours or on the weekend for a specified period.
- ❏ *Due process.* As used in schools, this refers to the procedures and processes that must be carried out before a student is deprived of privileges or rights.
- ❏ *Expulsion.* Removal of a student's right to attend school for a longer period of time, usually a semester or a year.
- ❏ *Felony.* A more serious criminal offense.
- ❏ *Hazing.* Mental or physical abuse to students as "initiation rites."
- ❏ *Misdemeanor.* A less serious criminal offense.
- ❏ *Procedural due process.* Extensive legalistic procedures required before depriving a student of a significant right or privilege, such as expulsion from school for an entire year.
- ❏ *Reasonable suspicion.* The degree of evidence that requires school personnel to notify police or child protection authorities of suspected child abuse.
- ❏ *Regime of voluntary inquiry.* The status of school libraries that renders unconstitutional the removal of books with unpopular ideas.

❏ *School disruption.* The standard used to judge the constitutionality of various issues involving student freedom of speech such as dress codes and student publication regulations.

❏ *Search and seizure rules.* A term applied to the rules the courts have established for law enforcement dealing with Fourth Amendment rights; school officials are given greater leeway to protect students.

❏ *Substantive due process.* More informal, "fair play" procedures required before depriving a student of a lesser right or privilege—for example, a one-day suspension from school.

❏ *Suspension.* Removal of a student's right to attend school for a short period of time, usually one or two days.

❏ *Truancy.* Failure to attend school as prescribed by compulsory education laws; a certain number of unexcused absences.

References

Banks v. Board of Public Instruction, 314 F. Supp. 285 (1970).

Bethel School District v. Fraser, 478 U.S. 675, 106 S.Ct. 3159, 92 L.Ed. 2d 549 (1986).

Board of Education v. Pico, 457 U.S. 853, 102 S.Ct. 2799, 73 L.Ed. 2d 435 (1982).

Burnside v. Byers, 363 F.2d 594 (5th Cir. 1956).

Dixon v. Alabama State, 294 F.2d 150 (5th Cir. 1961).

Goss v. Lopez, U.S. 565, 95 S.Ct. 729 (1975).

Grayned v. City of Rockford, 408 U.S. 104 (1972).

Guzick v. Drebus, 431 F.2d 594 (6th Cir. 1970).

Landeros v. Flood, 17 Cal.3d 399 (1975).

Mandel v. Municipal Court, 276 Cal. App. 2d. 649 (1970).

New Jersey v. T.L.O., 105 S.Ct. 733 (1985).

O'Rourke v. Walker, 102 Conn. 130, 128 A.25 (1925).

Solomon, D., Watson, M., Delucchi, K., Schaps, E., & Battistich, V. (1988). Enhancing children's prosocial behavior in the classroom. *American Educational Research Journal, 25*(4), 527-554.

Tinker v. Des Moines I.C.S.D., 393 U.S. 503, 506 (1969).

West Virginia State Board of Education v. Barnette, 319 U.S. 624 (1943).

5

Making the Campus Safe

5.1 A Duty to Protect

School officials have a fundamental duty to protect students. Through the years, the courts have recognized this duty by granting school administrators broad latitude to act quickly and decisively in protecting or defending the children in their charge. Although individual students are afforded the constitutional guarantees of all citizens, the courts recognize the necessity to abridge these rights when the safety and well-being of the student body is at stake. In Chapter 4, for example, we noted that school officials are not held to the same standards for search and seizure as law enforcement officers. Similarly, the courts and legislatures have endowed school administrators with ample authority to deal with those who would interfere with the process of schooling or who would pose a danger to the students.

Over the years, the legal duty to supervise and protect students has become a well-established principle. Consequently, lawsuits against districts failing to provide adequate supervision have resulted in hefty monetary awards. Sound administrative planning includes careful attention to the basic duty of school officials to protect students.

5.2 Avoiding Negligence

In the school setting, negligence generally means the school officials have not taken reasonable precautions to prevent injury to students or other citizens attending the school or using the school facilities. For a negligence claim to be sustained, the courts require four conditions to exist:

- First, there must be a legal *duty* to protect others from unreasonable risks of injury.
- Second, there must be a *breach* of that duty.
- Third, the breach must cause an *injury*.
- And, fourth, *damages* must be suffered as a result.

The legal duty of school administrators to provide a safe school environment for their students has been clearly mandated by the legislatures of the states and has been repeatedly reinforced by the courts.

5.3 Providing Adequate Supervision

At the top of a school administrator's list of duties relating to student safety is supervision. The courts will ask three questions to evaluate the judgment of school officials concerning supervision:

(1) Were any staff members assigned to supervise the area? School administrators are obliged to control and supervise all areas of the campus where students might congregate. Even if a danger was unforeseeable, the school district will probably be held responsible for accidents that might have been avoided if supervision had been present.

(2) Was the number of assigned supervisors sufficient? Assigning one campus supervisor to a large campus with many visual obstructions will not protect a school district from a charge of negligence, especially if the supervisor was not immediately present when the injury occurred. To ensure adequate supervision, an administrator must take into consideration the physical features of the facility to be supervised as well as the number of students.

(3) Were the assigned staff members adequately supervising? Staff members assigned to supervision must remain vigilant to stop potentially dangerous situations from developing. If the teachers on duty are congregated on one end of the playground chatting, the supervision is inadequate no matter how many staff members are assigned. School districts may even be held liable for accidents that occur off campus if they occurred because the school failed to provide supervision that could have prevented the young students from wandering off (*Hoyem v. Manhattan Beach City School District,* 1978).

We advise that school administrators add staff training to their yearly supervision plans. At minimum, staff should be schooled in four principles:

Principle 1: The obligation to report to the assigned supervision area on time. Administrators cannot be certain that their plans for adequate supervision are being carried out unless staff members accept their responsibilities seriously.

Principle 2: The necessity to stay alert and keep a watchful eye on the supervision area. The supervisors must constantly look for potentially dangerous activities, objects, equipment, and so on.

Principle 3: The duty to act in the event of a dangerous situation. The supervisors must act quickly to break up fights and prevent students from wandering off campus. Teachers and administrators do not have the luxury of ignoring a dangerous situation—even if it is personally uncomfortable.

Principle 4: A clear understanding of the authority of a teacher assigned to supervision. In many cases, a school supervisor carrying out the duty to protect students has more power and authority than the police. As the circumstances warrant, supervisors should not hesitate to call on law enforcement. Police officers enjoy the greater freedom they have when working with school officials.

5.4 Statute of Limitations and Administrative Claims

Under state laws, a person who intends to file a lawsuit against a school district must do so within a specified period of time and usually is required to file a claim in the district first. The claim must be filed within six months after the injury or damage occurs. This has been interpreted by the courts to mean six months from the time the person discovers that he or she has been injured. For example, a student or school employee may discover a year later the delayed effects of exposure to certain substances in the school environment or a chronic emotional reaction may develop from a seemingly harmless playground accident.

5.5 Dealing With Police

Police and other law enforcement officials have the absolute *right* to enter a public school campus, at any time, to question or arrest students or school personnel. Usually the police officers find it advantageous to work cooperatively with school officials. Accordingly, they normally contact the administration and conform to school procedures. It is important, however, that administrators recognize that cooperation with law enforcement is mandatory. School personnel do not have a right to be present with the student when questioned by the police, although the officers often allow this.

Police officers have the right to take students into custody without the permission of the school officials. When this happens, however, common sense (and, in many cases, state law) requires the school administrator to inform the parents immediately. Typically, school districts have procedures for dealing with law enforcement officers on campus. We advise that all members of the administrative staff, including clerical staff, be acquainted with these procedures. In the absence of district procedures, the site administrator should develop site procedures, taking care to be certain they are consistent with the state's laws.

5.6 Athletic Program Liability

Traditionally, the courts have ruled that students who elect to participate in athletics assume inherent risks. Consequently, unless the plaintiff can show negligence by the coach or the school, damages may not be recovered as the result of injuries.

Negligence on the part of coaches and school officials most frequently falls into four main categories:

(a) failure to provide and/or maintain safe equipment and facilities,
(b) failure to provide sufficient supervision,
(c) failure to properly teach the rules of the game or activity (including advice about various dangers), and
(d) willful and wanton misconduct by the coach or staff member.

School officials have an obligation to provide safe equipment and facilities. Furthermore, they must inspect the facilities and equipment on a regular basis to assure that they remain safe. Close supervision of athletic activities by knowledgeable personnel, coupled with careful attention to rules for "playing safely," are the school administrator's best bet for avoiding a costly lawsuit and bad publicity. We advise that the site administrator meet yearly with the school's coaches to review the basics of conducting a safe athletic program.

5.7 Physical Education Classes

Although many of the principles of conducting a safe athletic program also apply to required physical education classes, the students involved usually do not voluntarily elect to take these classes. Therefore the student does not "assume the risks." School officials must carefully select games and activities that are relatively safe. Naturally, any physical activity has inherent dangers, but such sports as tackle football or boxing should be banned from the physical education curriculum. Likewise, rough-house versions of legitimate sports, such as "jungle basketball," also must be banned. Trampolines have also been outlawed by most school districts because of the high liability insurance premiums required.

We advise that school officials review curriculum and procedures with the physical education staff periodically. The review should include four topics:

(a) potentially dangerous games and activities in the curriculum,
(b) strategies for teaching safe play and avoiding potential hazards,
(c) strategies for adequate supervision, and
(d) safety status of equipment and facilities.

5.8 Liability in Shop Classes

School officials are required to provide a safe learning environment in shop classes. Because these facilities are filled with potentially dangerous equipment, additional precautions must be taken.

First, the shop should be set up so that the instructor can adequately supervise student activities at all times. If this isn't possible, we advise that certain portions of the shop be closed. Safety is the first consideration.

Second, regular inspection of the facilities and equipment, including the safety devices, is essential. A checklist procedure is wise.

Third, essential in the eyes of the court is the school's obligation to teach its students to operate the shop equipment safely (*Paulsen v. Unified School Dist. No. 368*, 1986; *Velmer v. Baraga Area Schools*, 1988). This should be part of the written as well as the taught curricula.

5.9 Liability in Science Labs

Of the 5,000 school-related accidents reported annually, 3,200 occur in science labs. Specific recommendations to avoid lawsuits fall into four main categories:

- *Security*—adequate labeling and secure storing of both chemicals and equipment
- *Facilities*—safe and appropriate for instructional purposes with regular inspections
- *Protection*—protective goggles and clothing provided and required
- *Instruction*—age appropriate, with emphasis on safety

Sullivan (1990) lists the most common liability issues as failing to carry out supervisory obligations, failing to provide safety instructions, and failing to eliminate safety hazards. These three are common factors in most liability situations.

5.10 Liability on Playgrounds

Playground injuries are increasingly commonplace, with many due to poorly inspected or hazardous equipment. In 1990, the *Executive Educator* reported 16 bleacher collapses since 1978 with one injuring 83 students (Editor, 1990). Off-campus injuries, if caused by faulty instruction or equipment, underscore the school's responsibility to adequately train employees and thoroughly inspect off-campus activity sites.

5.11 Dealing With Loiterers and Other Outsiders

Maintaining a safe campus includes efforts to prevent outsiders from entering the school property and endangering the students. The advent of off-campus drug dealers has made this a major problem during the past two decades. In recent years, several states have armed school administrators with new laws to help them deal more effectively with outsiders. In California, for example, a trespasser may be fined up to $500 and jailed for up to six months if he or she refuses to leave the school when ordered to do so by the principal. Moreover, the law specifies that it must only *appear* to the principal that the person's presence would *likely* interfere with the peaceful conduct of the activities of the campus. Most states have similar laws to assist administrators in dealing with persons loitering near schools.

In general, it is not necessary for a school authority to wait until the crime has actually occurred to take action against loiterers or outsiders entering the campus. The laws and the courts support the duty of school officials to protect their students. Our advice is to act quickly and decisively to prevent loiterers from congregating around the campus and interlopers from entering. Become familiar with the state's penal codes and education code sections dealing with such matters. Provide excerpts of these codes on handy wallet-sized cards to all administrators and campus supervisors. These are particularly helpful when trouble arises and police are called. Reviewing the excerpted code sections with the responding police officers helps them form a basis for their action.

We also advise that school officials meet with the local police to determine in advance how the police will respond. Coordinated school-police efforts can reap big dividends in emergency situations.

Key Terms

❏ *Adequate supervision.* The conditions that exist when a sufficient number of properly trained staff are assigned to supervise student activities.

❏ *Injury and damages.* Suffering and loss caused by another person's actions or negligence.

❏ *Negligence.* A term used in the school setting to describe the failure to take reasonable precautions to prevent injury to students or citizens using school facilities.

❏ *Statute of limitations.* The time period within which a person who intends to file a lawsuit against the school district must do so.

References

Editor. (1990, March). Front lines. *Executive Educator, 12* (3), 7.
Hoyem v. Manhattan Beach City School District, 22 Cal.3d 508 (1978).
Paulsen v. Unified School Dist. No. 368, 717 P.2d 1051 (Kan. 1986)
Sullivan, R. L. (1990). 16 ways to lawyer-proof your lab. *Vocational Education Journal, 65*(2), 20, 22, 42.
Velmer v. Baraga Area Schools, 424 N.W.2d 770 (Mich. 1988).

6

Administering Special Education: The Question of Equal Access

6.1 Education for All Handicapped Children Act

For once, the U.S. Congress stepped out in front of the Supreme Court by passing the landmark Education for All Handicapped Children Act of 1975 (now the Individuals with Disabilities Education Act). Public Law 94-142, as it is commonly called, focused specifically on the nation's schools and demanded equal access for handicapped children. Since then, all states in the Union have adopted laws regulating special education for the handicapped. In many instances, state laws are even more stringent than PL 94-142 in the demand on their schools to provide equal access.

A. *Free Appropriate Education*

Included in the law is a definition of *free appropriate education*. Under this provision, public schools must provide special education and related services that meet certain requirements:

- they have been provided at public expense, under public supervision and direction, and without charge;
- they meet the standards of the state educational agency;
- they include an appropriate preschool, elementary, or secondary school education; and
- they are provided in conformity with an individualized educational program (IEP).

B. *Related Services*

Related services have been defined to include transportation and such developmental, corrective, and other support services including speech pathology and audiology, psychological services, physical and occupational therapy, recreation, and medical and counseling services. Medical services are only required for diagnostic and evaluation purposes.

C. *The Limits of the School's Responsibility*

Since the passage of the Education for All Handicapped Children Act, the Supreme Court has considered a spate of cases resulting in a new set of guidelines for public schools across the nation.

In the landmark *Rowley* case (*Board of Education v. Rowley*, 1982), the Supreme Court clarified the concept of "free and appropriate education." The Court ruled that PL 94-142 does not require the school to "maximize" the potential of each handicapped student. In rejecting the parents' request for the school to pay for a special sign language interpreter to help their deaf child, the Court declared that the school need only provide sufficient personalized instruction and support services to permit the handicapped student to benefit educationally from the instruction.

In support of a parental request for related services, the Supreme Court ruled that the school is required to provide "school health services" if they are necessary to allow a handicapped student to benefit from instruction. The Court distinguished between "medical services" that must be performed by medical personnel and "school health services" that may be performed by a school nurse or other qualified personnel normally found on the school campus. In one case, the school was ordered to provide routine catheterization to an 8-year-old student born with spina bifida.

D. *The Individual Educational Program (IEP)*

An important component of a handicapped student's access to public education is the individual educational program (IEP), which is designed by the school staff in consultation with the parents. If the school district is unable to offer an appropriate public special education program as defined by the IEP, the district must provide an appropriate private school placement at no cost to the parents (*Burlington School Committee v. Department of Education of Massachusetts,* 1985). The law also provides that parents must be notified of their right to participate in the design of their child's individual educational program. Likewise, they must be notified of assessment and placement procedures and of any contemplated change in the placement as well as their right to due process to resolve disagreements with the district.

Many state educational codes require a school district to provide additional specific services and programs. These should also be included in notifications to parents. Local administrators should consult with special education staff of the state department of education to be certain that all federal and state laws pertaining to parent notification and participation are observed.

E. Suspension and Expulsion of Handicapped Students

The Supreme Court has held that long-term suspension or expulsion of handicapped students amounts to "changes in placement" under the Education of the Handicapped Act and therefore requires full IEP modification procedures. Recognizing the necessity for school officials to protect the safety of other students, the Court ruled that administrators may temporarily suspend handicapped students for up to 10 days without violating the provisions of the law. Handicapped students may not be expelled for conduct caused by the handicapping condition.

F. Fair Hearing

The Individuals with Disabilities Education Act (IDEA) mandates certain procedures to guarantee the rights of handicapped students. Foremost among these is the right to an impartial hearing before a hearing officer who is affiliated neither with the district nor with the state department of education. During the period of time the hearing is pending, the student must remain in his or her current program. Following the hearing procedure, in some states, the parent has a right to appeal to the state department of education and finally to either the state or the federal court system. If the parents prevail at the administrative or judicial level, the law provides that they be awarded attorney's fees.

G. Placement of Handicapped Students: Mainstreaming

The IDEA requires that handicapped children be educated in the least restrictive environment. That is, whenever possible, they should be educated with nonhandicapped children in regular classrooms. Disputes between parents and school districts often arise over the appropriateness of an individual educational program that prescribes all or part of the student's education in segregated facilities for the handicapped. The courts have ruled that the current law's preference for mainstreaming (reflecting present-day special education philosophy) must be tempered by the possibility that some students will be better off in segregated facilities. By no means does this relieve the school administrator from the obligation to creatively research school resources to provide handicapped students with a free and appropriate education. On the contrary, the courts routinely judge the efforts of the staff in working with the parents to enable the students to receive educational benefits (*Lachman v. Illinois Board of Education,* 1988). The courts also scrutinize the duties of the school district in complying with the procedures spelled out in the law, including various notifications to parents. Consequently, many administrators feel it is wise to document these various procedures and notifications through registered mail.

6.2 School Year for Handicapped

The IDEA also requires that, where necessary for handicapped children to benefit from special education, the district must provide an extended school year, usually an extra month. School districts also may be required to educate handicapped students beyond the usual 18-year-old limit, up to age 21 (*Natrona County School District v. McKnight,* 1988).

6.3 IQ Tests for Placement

In many states, including California, IQ tests may not be administered to black children to identify handicaps because the tests tend to identify a high percentage of minority students as handicapped, resulting in racially imbalanced classes.

Key Terms

❑ *Education for All Handicapped Children Act of 1975 (now the Individuals with Disabilities Education Act).* The federal law that established stringent requirements for school districts to provide access for handicapped children to public education.

❑ *Fair hearing.* Due process procedures mandated by the Education for All Handicapped Children Act to guarantee the rights of handicapped students.

❑ *Free public education.* The obligation of public schools to provide individualized services to handicapped children free of charge.

❑ *Individualized educational program (IEP).* The specialized program of study and services formulated with the advice of parents to meet the handicapped child's extraordinary needs.

❑ *Mainstreaming.* A practice of placing handicapped students in regular classes so that they are educated in "the least restrictive environment."

❑ *Related services.* Additional noneducational services provided to handicapped children to facilitate access to education, including transportation, speech pathology, audiology, psychological services, and a variety of therapies.

References

Board of Education v. Rowley, 458 U.S. 176, 102 S.Ct. 3034 (1982).

Burlington School Committee v. Department of Education of Massachusetts, 471 U.S. 359, 105 S.Ct. 1996, 85 L.Ed 2d 385 (1985).

Lachman v. Illinois Board of Education, 852 F.2d 290 (7th Cir. 1988).

Natrona County School District v. McKnight, 764 P.2d 1039 (Wyo. 1988).

7

Coping With Legal Problems in Personnel Management

There is no shortage of laws regarding the many aspects of personnel management: hiring, teacher evaluation, tenure, due process rights, personnel files, and contract and salary administration. Except in rare cases, however, the law is clear and based on fairness. Dos and don'ts regarding the six personnel management areas identified above are presented in this chapter.

7.1 Hiring Professional Staff

The following is a list of major federal laws affecting hiring practices:

- Title VII of the Civil Rights Act of 1964: prohibits discrimination on the basis of race, color, religion, gender, or national origin
- Age Discrimination in Employment Act of 1968
- Equal Pay Act of 1963
- Rehabilitation Act of 1973

These laws, their amendments, and the resulting case laws have resulted in direct implications for hiring practices regarding race, name, age, religion, sex, ethnic background, marital or family status, and life-style.

A. Race

It is legal to request information about distinguishing physical characteristics but illegal to ask the color of the applicant's skin, eyes, and so on, if the intent of the question is to determine race or color.

Implication. There are no justifiable reasons for asking such questions. So don't ask them and avoid discrimination charges.

B. Name

Questions regarding an applicant's name are legal if the information is needed to verify work or education records received by your office. It is unlawful, however, to use such questions to determine ancestry or national origin.

Implication. Unless there is an obvious inconsistency regarding applicants' names in their data files, don't ask questions about applicants' names. There is little or nothing to gain and a lot to lose.

C. Age

As far as the law is concerned, questions about age are taboo. In the law's opinion, a qualified teacher is a qualified teacher is a qualified teacher, regardless of age.

Implication. Don't inquire about age. As with race and name, you have little to gain and a lot to lose. An exception is requiring proof of age in the form of a work permit or birth certificate. These situations are generally limited to nonprofessional positions.

D. *Religion*

All inquiries are illegal.

Implication. Don't ask questions regarding or related to religion.

E. *Sex*

Questions are legitimate only when a true occupational requirement exists.

Implication. We know of no job in a school or school district where a true occupational gender requirement exists. If you think you've found one, check with legal counsel or the appropriate supervisor before taking action. In the meantime, make no inquiries regarding sex or sexual preferences.

F. *Marital and Family Status*

Questions regarding marital status (e.g., married? single? divorced?) are illegal. In special circumstances, questions about the applicant's ability to meet a certain work schedule are lawful.

Implication. Don't ask questions about the applicant's marital status.

G. *Life-Style*

What an employee does during nonschool time is personal business. Questions about drinking alcoholic beverages or taking drugs are illegal. Asking questions about future career plans is legitimate, however.

Questions have recently arisen about teacher out-of-school behavior. There was a time when school boards could set restrictive dress codes, disallow marriage and consumption of alcoholic beverages, and so on. Those days have passed. Teachers' and other school employees' private lives are their own business unless they

disrupt the smooth operation of the school or
impair their effectiveness at work.

Questions about the appropriateness of questionable behaviors should be cleared by legal counsel or appropriate higher supervisors.

The message is clear. Questions regarding an applicant's or employee's age, name, sex, religion, race, marital status, and life-style have no legitimate role in the workplace. And it makes sense. As a potential employer, your concern is the applicant's qualifications for the job. Questions regarding these aspects of applicants' lives have little or no impact on their ability to perform their job. Avoid questions in these areas and stick to questions that are designed to ascertain the *ability to fulfill the job requirements* of the position in question.

7.2 Teacher Evaluation

Teacher evaluation is required in all states and is governed by district policies, bargaining agreements, and state laws. Information gained from personnel evaluations plays a role in making many decisions: tenure, performance rewards, merit pay, professional development plans and programs, and dismissal.

All of these are very important, but the primary purpose is and must be instructional improvement. The other decisions are secondary.

The key to successful teacher evaluation is *complying with the district teacher evaluation policy.* This advice is based on the assumption that the district policy and evaluation program are in compliance with state law and the bargaining agreement.

Without strict compliance, due process will not be followed, and the information gathered will be subject to grievance procedures.

7.3 Tenure

Tenure gives the recipients a very strong property interest in their jobs and is protected by due process. This is the basic difference between probationary teachers and tenured teachers. Probationary teachers have no property interest in their employment or due process rights. Their employment can be terminated at the end of their contract after meeting minimal due process provisions. In contrast, a tenured teacher cannot be terminated without following all provisions of due process.

7.4 Due Process Rights of Employees

These rights are employment protections given to employees against wrongful dismissal or suspension of pay. Two categories of due process affect dismissal cases: substantive due process and procedural due process. Definitions of each and related guidelines are provided below.

A. Substantive Due Process

Substantive due process requires administrators to provide valid reasons and substantial supporting evidence for termination to prevent arbitrary and capricious dismissal.

Guidelines

- Provide your employees with written and oral standards of performance.
- Provide documented evidence of substandard performance.
- Offer resource assistance to help the employee eliminate deficiencies.
- Specify opportunities available to improve job performance.

B. *Procedural Due Process*

Procedural due process requires school administrators to follow constitutional procedures regarding notices and hearings.

Guidelines

- Provide
    notice of charges/procedures/rights,
    an opportunity for a hearing,
    an unbiased decision maker, and
    hearing process rights including the right to legal counsel, to examine witnesses, to call witnesses to testify, and to examine written records.
- Follow state statutory and local policies and procedures including time lines.

Due process requirements vary slightly from state to state and can be augmented by employee contracts or district policy. Be sure to review all of these to ensure compliance. A detailed description of due process as it relates to dismissal is provided in another book in this series, *Maximizing People Power in Schools* (Frase, 1992).

The superintendent of schools generally is authorized by policy to suspend employees with pay. Details regarding this procedure are found in state law, policy, and contract agreements.

7.5 Personnel Files

A. *Contents*

A file should be kept in the district office for every district employee. The file should contain all records related to the employee such as employee evaluations, growth plans and recommendations, complaints, and commendations. Although it differs from state to state and province to province, administrators are generally not permitted to place complaints or other derogatory comments regarding the employee in the personnel file without first offering the employee an opportunity to review the material. The employee has the right to place a rebuttal in the file.

The file should also contain certificates and other employment licenses, academic records, preemployment records, and application forms. All documents should be kept in one file.

B. Access

Personnel files are private. Only school officials or their designees, the employee, review panels or others authorized by the employee, and court personnel may have access to them. This means that parents, students, other employees, and other community officials do not have a right to review them.

With the exception of their preemployment records, employees have the right to review their files during regular business hours and in an area designated by the superintendent. Because employees have the right to inspect their files and have a reasonable expectation that all personnel information of substance will be found there, it is mandatory that all personnel records for each employee be kept in one file. Experienced personnel officers advise that preemployment records be kept in a separate envelope marked "confidential," which should be removed from the file before inspection by the employee. Any information presented by the district at a trial or hearing but not previously available in the file for the employee's review can be stricken from the record and not authorized for use in the hearing or trial.

7.6 Contracts and Salary

The contract agreement between the employee association and the board of education specifies a process for determining salaries for all employees. The reader is advised to review the contract(s) carefully and to act in compliance with its provisions at all times. If changes in the contract are needed, they must be instituted through the bargaining process. Districts in states that do not require collective bargaining are exempt from this rule; however, caution is advised. Changing compensation plans is a sure way to incite hostility.

Being intimately familiar with the contract is absolutely crucial. You can bet the teacher association representatives are, and they will not hesitate to file grievances and attempt to discredit you when you fail to act in accordance with it.

In general, the contract states the rights and responsibilities of both the employees and the employer. More about contract management is presented in Chapter 8, "Avoiding the Legal Pitfalls of Collective Bargaining."

7.7 Worker's Compensation

Worker's compensation is a form of disability insurance for employees and is mandated by the states. Benefits are subject to the legislative process, and worker's compensation programs are administered by the appropriate state authorities. Disability payments are determined in accordance with minimum and maximum payment schedules determined at the state level and the employee's current salary, future earnings, and financial responsibilities.

Funding for worker's compensation programs is borne entirely by the school district. The method of providing worker's compensation insurance is usually left to the discretion of the employer, who may purchase it from private or public companies or provide the protection through pooled funds of a self-insuring program. The cost of worker's compensation is determined primarily by the school district's track record with claims.

The key is to ensure that your work environment is safe, clean, and free of potential hazards that might inflict harm on employees, such as asbestos, contaminated drinking water, uneven sidewalks, poor lighting, improper storage of chemicals, and unsafe tools and equipment. More about risk management is presented in Chapter 9, "Strategies to Avoid Lawsuits."

Key Terms

❑ *Job discrimination.* An illegal act wherein a person is denied employment or due process on the basis of age, gender, race, and so on without a rational basis.

❑ *Personnel file.* The file in which an employee's personnel records are kept; access to this file is limited to the employee, the supervisors, and the courts.

❑ *Probationary status.* The status of employment that precedes tenure; it does not provide due process protections given to tenured teachers.

❑ *Procedural due process.* Procedures required in the dismissal process: notice of deficiency, right to unbiased decision maker, hearing process rights, and adherence to time lines.

❑ *Teacher evaluation policy.* A policy that governs evaluation of personnel.

❑ *Tenure.* Employment status extended to teachers to protect them from arbitrary and capricious discipline and dismissal; it is a property interest protected by due process requirements.

❑ *Wrongful dismissal.* Using inappropriate reasons or incorrect procedures for terminating employment.

Reference

Frase, L. E. (1992). *Maximizing people power in schools.* Newbury Park, CA: Corwin.

8

Avoiding the Legal Pitfalls of Collective Bargaining

8.1 The Legal Foundations of Collective Bargaining

Collective bargaining is a fairly recent arrival on the educational scene. Since before the turn of the century, workers in the private sector were involved in collective bargaining of one sort or another. The courts accepted the right of labor to organize and bargain as part of the laissez-faire political economic system. In those early years, the courts generally sided with management when strikes, picketing, or slowdowns caused economic damage to companies or to the community. The result was oppressive court injunctions, and the union movement in the

United States was stifled considerably. In 1932, Congress turned the tables by passing the Norris-LaGuardia Act, which forbid federal courts from using the injunction against union activities resulting from labor disputes. Several states immediately followed suit, and today modern labor laws only allow courts to use injunctions if specific laws are broken or if the nation's security is threatened. The following is a checklist of tips for developing sound contract management:

- Know your contract. Every administrator must be aware of the spirit and intent of each contract provision. This takes time, but it pays off.
- Make contract administration a team effort. Spend time with coadministrators discussing contract management issues and strategies.
- Establish contract management training for new administrators and continuing administrators. The emphasis should be on perpetuating a uniform, consistent contract management strategy.
- Base your personnel decisions on principles of fair play.
- Comply with the letter and spirit of the contract.
- Develop a grievance council to review employee concerns and advise the supervisors involved. This requires administrators and union leadership who are secure enough to allow rank and file teacher participation in the governance of the school or district. Naturally, both sides of the bargaining table must agree to the formation and operation of an employee council empowered to deal with employer-employee relations.

A. *The National Labor Relations Act*

In 1935, the United States became the first nation on earth to institutionalize collective bargaining. The National Labor Relations Act (the Wagner Act) established a legal framework for private sector collective bargaining. It established the National Labor Relations Board and charged it with the responsibility to regulate unions and to deal with unfair labor practices. It established a legal obligation for both labor and management to bargain in good faith.

Up to this time, collective bargaining had been limited to the private sector, and many of the champions of the union movement during the Depression believed that the principles of collective bargaining could not work in the public sector. President Franklin Roosevelt, for example, was a strong supporter of organized labor but maintained steadfastly that collective bargaining "cannot be transplanted into the public service."

B. Collective Bargaining for Public Employees

The rationale for excluding public employees from participating in collective bargaining was a belief that, in a democracy, the people are sovereign; consequently, the decisions of their elected officials must be sovereign. In other words, by giving away the absolute authority of elected officials to make decisions for the people, the right of the people to govern themselves would be compromised. Modern-day critics tend to down play the theoretical loss of power by the people and focus more on the practical differences between the public and the private sectors. Economic forces such as profitability and competition, which bear on industrial employers but do not bear on governmental employers, present real dilemmas to political theorists.

More than twenty years after the Congress sanctioned collective bargaining for private sector workers, Wisconsin became the first state to grant collective bargaining rights to teachers. Within three years, President Kennedy signed an Executive Order giving limited collective bargaining rights to federal employees and, within the next two decades, 32 states had adopted collective bargaining laws for teachers and other public employees.

C. The Right to Strike for Teachers

The right to strike is considered by most labor leaders to be an essential part of collective bargaining. They believe that, without strikes, effective negotiations would be reduced to a meaningless exercise. Nevertheless, the collective bargaining laws for teachers in most states prohibit strikes. Striking is expressly permitted only after all other procedures have failed in Alaska, Hawaii, Minnesota, Montana, Oregon, Pennsylvania, Vermont, and Wisconsin. In some states, the law is silent on the matter; in other states, a mechanism for impasse resolution has been adopted (binding arbitration, for example). In California, one of the states whose law is silent on the question of teachers' right to strike, the state supreme court ruled that strikes by teachers in the state were not illegal, because no law prohibiting them existed. This ruling diminished the threat of court injunction and cleared the way for numerous teacher strikes in the state.

Today, the vast majority of teachers throughout the nation are members of units that bargain collectively with the local school boards. The pattern and protocols for the bargaining process have been borrowed from the private sector. Some observers have suggested that today's developments in public school labor relations parallel those of the private sector in the early years (Alexander & Alexander, 1985).

D. *Exclusive Representation*

A fundamental element in all collective bargaining processes is the selection of an exclusive bargaining representative. This is accomplished by an election, usually conducted by the committee of state officials in charge of regulating collective bargaining (the state equivalent to the National Labor Relations Board). The representative is normally an affiliate of one of the large national unions, the National Education Association (NEA) or the American Federation of Teachers (AFT). It also can be an independent local teachers organization, however. Once the exclusive representative has been identified, it assumes the obligation to represent all teachers, whether they are members of the organization or not.

Similar processes are conducted for the noncertified members of the staff. Usually the unions involved are affiliates of the American Federation of Labor-Congress of Industrial Organizations (AFL-CIO). Often the noncertified staff is clustered into more than one bargaining unit, frequently represented by more than one union. For example, the secretarial-clerical staff may form a bargaining unit and elect a union that primarily represents office employees or state employees. District maintenance personnel, carpenters, and plumbers, on the other hand, would probably form a separate bargaining unit and affiliate with one of the trade unions. In any event, once the exclusive representative is elected by the bargaining unit, it is responsible for representing the interests of every member of that bargaining unit, including employees who choose not to belong to the union.

E. Scope of Bargaining

Scope of bargaining refers to those aspects of public school employment that the school board is required, by law, to put on the table when negotiating with the exclusive bargaining representative. In the private sector, these aspects are determined by the National Labor Relations Board (NLRB). They include wages, hours, terms, and conditions of employment. In most states, the scope of bargaining for school employees is spelled out in statute. Usually, the basic list is very similar to the NLRB's list: wages, hours, terms, and conditions of employment. Frequently, it is up to the state-level labor relations board to determine whether the school operations fall into categories that are bargainable. Some teachers associations, for example, argue that the curriculum should be negotiable as well as the number of students in the classroom.

High on the list of traditional concerns of teachers brought to the bargaining table are procedures for transfer, evaluation, promotion, and grievances. High on the list of concerns for union officials are agency fee, release time for union officers, and binding arbitration.

8.2 The Negotiating Process

Collective bargaining laws generally specify a process patterned after the one established by the National Labor Relations Act of 1935—with a few minor modifications to adapt the process for public agencies.

A. *Sunshining*

The first modification usually involves "sunshining" the initial bargaining proposals so that the public has a chance to inspect the issues before negotiations begin. This process really has little meaning, however, because both proposals contain a potpourri of requests and demands that are no more than "chips" to be bargained away in the negotiating process.

Following the required sunshining of the proposals, the two negotiating teams meet and establish a calendar of negotiation sessions.

Nothing in the collective bargaining laws requires school district negotiations to be held in public. Typically, they are held in private at the request of the unions.

The two negotiating teams are charged with the responsibility to bargain in good faith. At the end of two or three months of negotiations, a tentative agreement is usually produced. Once this tentative agreement has been accepted by the teachers association and adopted by the school board, the new contract is in force and the negotiation process ends.

B. *Impasse*

If the two teams fail to reach agreement, either side can ask the state-level labor relations board to declare an impasse.

C. *Mediation*

Following the declaration of impasse by the labor relations board, a mediator is assigned by the state to the negotiation process. The mediator attempts to counsel both parties and to suggest alternatives for breaking the impasse. Often, a mediator is able to clarify the real bottom-line issues and, in many cases, propose rational compromise packages that could not have been developed in the hostile arena of traditional adversarial negotiations.

D. Fact-Finding

If the mediation process is not successful, the next step is fact-finding. Although the name of this phase of negotiations suggests some sort of independent investigation, fact-finding is, in fact, simply a courtroom-style hearing of the arguments. The "fact-finder" is a hearing officer or law judge who hears the cases presented by the negotiators for each side (often attorneys). Once the cases are presented and the witnesses cross-examined, the fact-finder closes the hearing and writes his or her "findings." The fact-finder's recommendations are not binding on the school board.

E. Post-Fact-Finding Negotiations

Once the fact-finder's report has been released, the two negotiating teams are again obliged to meet for post-fact-finding negotiations. The purpose of these negotiations is to explore whether the objective fact-finder has added any insights that might bring about a settlement.

F. Arbitration

In some states, the law provides for an arbitrator to settle the dispute in the event the teachers union and the school board cannot reach a final settlement. In most cases, the arbitrator's decision must be one of the two "last best offers." In other words, after hearing the evidence and considering the argument, the arbitrator will rule in favor of the union or in favor of the district. "Splitting the difference" is not permitted. Theoretically, this procedure motivates the two sides to bargain reasonably and in good faith before going to arbitration. Outrageous demands, presumably, would cause the arbitrator to rule in favor of the other team's last best offer.

G. *Concerted Action*

After the mediation and fact-finding processes are over, unions in states where strikes are permitted are entitled to withhold services. As noted previously, in some states where strikes are not expressly permitted, the courts have ruled that work stoppages are not illegal and thus cannot be stopped by court action. It is important to note, however, that strikes and slowdowns are never sanctioned by labor relations boards or courts before the entire negotiation process has been exhausted —including mediation and fact-finding—unless provoked by an unfair labor practice. Complaints against unions that strike prematurely are usually supported by the labor relations boards. The unions are subsequently subject to substantial penalties.

H. *Union Security*

Unions negotiate with employers for various means to strengthen their positions with the bargaining units they represent. One of three arrangements is usually sought: agency fee, payroll deduction, or maintenance of membership.

I. *Agency Fee*

The agency fee is most advantageous for the union. It requires that all employees in the bargaining unit either join the union and pay dues or pay a "fee" roughly equivalent to the dues. The purpose of the fee is to require all employees to pay a fair share of the union's cost of representing the employees. The Supreme Court has ruled that the employee's nonunion fee cannot be calculated to include the cost of the union's political activities (*Chicago Teachers Union v. Hudson*, 1986). Consequently, in many states, the required fee for employees who choose not to join the union is approximately 10% to 30% less than membership dues.

8.3 Alternatives to Adversarial Bargaining

In recent years, many forward-thinking union leaders and school administrators have come to the conclusion that the model for negotiations borrowed from the 1930s industrial unions is not working well for public schools. Teachers and board members alike lament the loss of support for schools and teachers that has paralleled the collective bargaining movement in education. Students of public school negotiations remind us that collective bargaining laws do not *require* the industrial adversarial model. Rather, this is the mandated process in the event the union leaders and board members cannot devise a more sensible process. Many districts, throughout the nation, are experimenting with joint governance models that bring teacher leadership authentically into the management of the district. Other models are based on extensive "trust agreements" and delegate extensive authority to school site councils composed of teachers, administrators, and parents. Whatever the model, the principle seems to be greater employee involvement in the governance and administration of the school operations. As a result, the need for destructive, confrontational tactics is eliminated or at least significantly diminished.

8.4 Contract Management and Grievance Procedures

Commenting on the future of the United Auto Workers, one of the union's colorful outgoing presidents pointed out that union leaders don't build strong unions; company managers build strong unions. Whether the school district is involved with a progressive, cooperative labor relations model or a traditional adversarial model, the success of negotiations often lies in the hands of school administrators. The checklist on page 93 provides a framework for sound contract and grievance management.

Key Terms

❏ *Agency fee.* A requirement that all employees in the bargaining unit either join the union and pay dues or pay a "fee" roughly equivalent to the dues.

❏ *Contract arbitration.* A process carried out by an arbitrator to judge the merits of grievances pertaining to the contract.

❏ *Exclusive representative.* A union or association that by election has been granted the exclusive right to represent a group of employees in negotiations with the management.

❏ *Fact-finding.* A hearing before a hearing officer resulting in a judgment and usually a recommendation on the "facts" presented.

❏ *Impasse.* Failure of the two negotiating teams to reach an agreement, usually certified by the state-level labor relations board.

❏ *Mediation.* A process conducted by a mediator who attempts to counsel both negotiating teams for the purpose of breaking an impasse.

❏ *National Labor Relations Act (Wagner Act).* Federal law that established a legal framework for private sector collective bargaining in 1935.

❏ *National Labor Relations Board.* The board established by the National Labor Relations Act to oversee private sector bargaining. The NLRB has been used as a model for public school collective bargaining laws.

❏ *Scope of bargaining.* Those aspects of employment that the school board or management is required by law to negotiate with the exclusive bargaining representative.

❏ *Strike.* A concerted action by an employees union to withhold services.

❏ *Sunshining (public notice).* An opportunity for public inspection of bargaining proposals.

❏ *Union security.* A term usually applied to negotiated arrangements with management for closed shop, agency fee, payroll deduction of dues, or maintenance of membership.

References

Alexander, K., & Alexander, D. (1985). *American public school law.* St. Paul, MN: West.

Chicago Teachers Union v. Hudson, 475 U.S. 292 (1986).

9

Strategies to Avoid Lawsuits

9.1 Planning With the Courts in Mind

Much of the work of educational administrators is often described as "crisis management." Administrators frequently complain that they have lost control of their organizations. Effective managers, however, have always been described as proactive: anticipating behaviors leading to potential disaster and devising policies and procedures to deal with each situation. This type of proactive planning is the essence of what has come to be known as *risk management*.

During the 1970s, educational organizations experienced an onslaught of litigation as society sought to effect social change through the courts. Such issues as fair hiring practices and dismissals joined personal injuries as frequent grounds for suing schools. As liability insurance became more and more expensive, many administrators attempted to avoid risk by eliminating potentially dangerous programs regardless of educational value or benefit to students. It was out of this chaos that risk management, a form of loss control, became an essential tool of supervisors at all levels.

9.2 Risk Management

Risk management has become a practical means of dealing with potential loss because it allows organizations to maintain marginally risky activities important to the educational institution instead of eliminating them. The art of risk management involves (a) identifying risks, (b) evaluating risks, (c) eliminating or reducing the risks, and (d) financing any remaining exposure. Financing risk may involve the acquisition of liability insurance, "pooling" potential loss, or even self-insuring.

A national survey taken in 1988 and reported by Underwood and Noffke in 1990 reported that the four most common types of lawsuits among educational systems, in order of their appearance, were (a) negligence, (b) employee dismissal, (c) contract negotiation or implementation, and (d) special education. The implications are obvious: By applying risk management strategies within our organizations, especially in the four high-risk areas mentioned above, we can significantly reduce the odds that our districts will be the targets of litigation. At the very least, school administrators are obliged to take preventive measures by reviewing current district policies and procedures to ensure adherence to legal requirements. Moreover, follow-up checks should be made to be sure policies and procedures are being observed. (For further discussion of the four high-risk lawsuit areas, see Chapter 5, "Making the Campus Safe"; Chapter 6, "Administering Special Education"; Chapter 7, "Coping With Legal Problems in Personnel Management"; and Chapter 8, "Avoiding the Legal Pitfalls of Collective Bargaining.")

The use of risk management strategies within education has implications for all levels of management. At the district level, policy formulation and communication are paramount. Following are tips for the superintendent:

1. Establish and promulgate rules and regulations dealing with potential risk factors and safety.
2. Establish necessary communication among all stakeholders: students, parents, community, and employee groups.
3. Provide internal communication about policies, laws, procedures, and potential risks.
4. Ensure that clear policy statements are formulated and distributed and that regulations are being consistently applied.
5. Employ knowledgeable people who know both their responsibilities and the extent of their authority.

As with most educational concerns, it is at the site level that policy meets performance. The principal or supervisor is vital in ensuring that a risk management program works.

9.3 The Role of the Principal in Risk Management

Principals are responsible for ensuring that risk management policies are consistently applied throughout the school by all employees and students. Although it is impossible to completely safeguard a school, certain strategies and procedures will both convey the message that safety is foremost as well as reduce the likelihood of injury. The following guidelines are basic:

- Organize school safety review committees to inspect, monitor, and report unsafe conditions as well as to recommend safety procedures.
- Conduct regular inspections of facilities and equipment.
- Facilitate safety maintenance requests.
- Arrange for staff development programs that include training in emergency procedures, first aid, and CPR.

- Emphasize the staff role in risk management (team approach).

As the safety and supervision of students is of the greatest importance, it is necessary for school administrators to err on the side of repetition in ensuring that both staff and students are aware of safety practices and procedures. Stern (1978) suggests the following guidelines:

- Conduct regular assemblies to explain and review safety rules.
- Make sure that the instructions account for student maturity levels.
- Make sure that each student is continuously supervised at all times during the school day.
- Ensure that all staff are assigned to appropriate duties and receive adequate training.
- Post warning signs where necessary to communicate potential risks.
- Make sure that off-campus activities have parental permission, principal approval, adequate instruction, and supervision.
- Designate a responsible person to assume authority in the principal's absence.

Most risk management involves common sense. By consistently promoting reasonable maintenance, safety instruction, supervision, and lawful practices, the school administrator practices risk management. The leaders of educational institutions have both a corporate and a public responsibility not to allow potential risks to corrupt sound pedagogy. The most efficacious means of ensuring this is to institutionalize the practice of risk management.

Key Terms

❑ *Pooling.* The technique of collaborating with other school districts and contributing funds to cover potential lawsuit losses.

❏ *Risk management.* An administrative planning process that combines loss control techniques, safety programs, and liability insurance to allow school districts to carry on minimally dangerous operations and educational activities.

❏ *Self-insuring.* The technique of setting aside funds to cover the eventuality of judgments against the district, in lieu of purchasing insurance.

References

Stern, R. D. (1978). The principal and tort liability. In *The school principal and the law.* Topeka, KS: National Organization on Legal Problems in Education.

Underwood, J. K., & Noffke, J. (1990). Good news: The litigation scales are tilting in your favor. In *Executive educator.* Alexandria, VA: National School Boards Association.

Troubleshooting Guide

Handicapped Children and Special Education Problems

NOTES